Rag Rug Creations

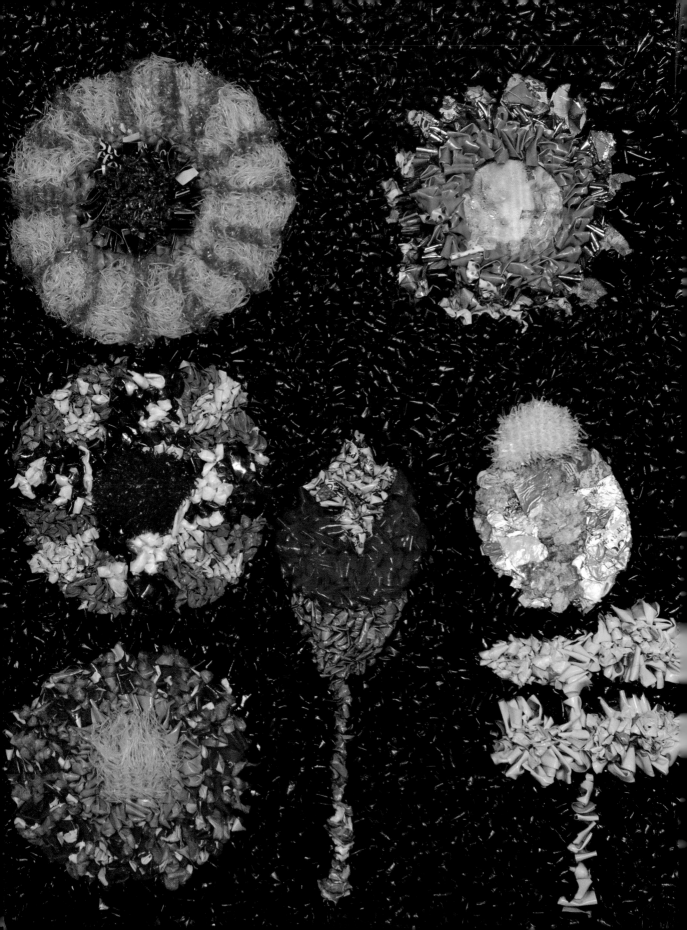

Rag Rug Creations

AN EXPLORATION OF COLOUR AND SURFACE

Lynne Stein

B L O O M S B U R Y

LONDON • NEW DELHI • NEW YORK • SYDNEY

Dedicated to my parents, Eileen and Bernie Margolis, in loving memory.

First published in Great Britain 2014
Bloomsbury Visual Arts
An imprint of Bloomsbury Publishing Plc
50 Bedford Square
London WC1B 3DP
www.bloomsbury.com

Bloomsbury is a registered trade mark of
Bloomsbury Publishing Plc.

ISBN: 9781408157565

Commissioning editor: Susan Kelly
Assistant editor: Agnes Upshall
Copy editor: Jane Anson
Series design: Sutchinda Thompson
Cover: Eleanor Rose
Page layouts: Susan McIntyre

Printed and bound in China

No responsibility or loss caused to any
individual or organisation acting on
or refraining from action as a result of
the material in this publication can be
accepted by Bloomsbury or the author.

A CIP catalogue record for this book is
available from the British Library

IMAGES
Front cover (clockwise from top): 'It's a
Wrap' box canvas picture; 'Mythological
Beast' wall hanging; 'Spotty Lovebird'
cushion.

Back cover: 'Gawthorpe's Jacobean Motifs'
wall hanging (detail).

Contents

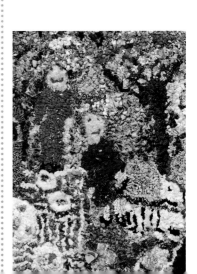

Introduction

My own enthusiasm for rug-hooking, and for rag rugs generally, comes from a variety of sources, and least of all from any claim to be a talented needlewoman! In fact, my art training was as an exhibition and display designer, and then, some years later, as an art therapist. Unlike many other makers and collectors of rag rugs, I have no known personal family history where rag rugs featured in our lives. However, my paternal family were textile traders, my grandmother's shops displaying a sumptuous array of buttons and trimmings. Some of my earliest memories, much to my parents' displeasure, are of unpicking and trying to work out the construction of the candlewick bedspreads which adorned our beds in a style typical of the 1950s.

My interests lie in the craft's history on both sides of the Atlantic, with its distinct contrasts, its folk-art culture and appearance, and its very inventive use of recycling. I have always been challenged and motivated by the notion of creating or refashioning 'something precious out of that which might otherwise have been discarded'.

As a child, I liked to investigate the process of combining different found materials and media: ribbons, string, papers, shoe polish, wax and paint. As a design student back in the late 1960s, I was making and selling hand-painted papier mâché buttons, brooches and buckles, to appear as fashionable accessories in the pages of glossy magazines. Creating marks, pictures, patterns and surfaces from juxtaposed units of looped or tufted colour and texture is what fascinates me as a maker. In this respect, the process of making rag rugs is comparable to mosaic, beadwork, collage, pointillism, and even

01 **Candace Bahouth, *Wentworth Chair*** *(detail), early 21st century. Mosaic.*

02 **Cleo Mussi, *Hot Dog (Pharma's Market)*,** *2009. 80 x 52 cm (31 ½ x 20 ½ in). Mosaic. Recycled crockery. Photograph by Peter J. Stone.*

02

7

the British tradition of well-dressing, where found materials also provide some of the interest and inspiration.

In the early 1980s I attended a weekend workshop led by Ali Rhind. The 'hookie' and 'proggie' techniques I was shown seemed to offer so much potential in terms of manipulating fabric and fibre, creating exciting textures, patterns and colour blends, and finding one's own unique and expressive way of working. Part of the appeal also was the immediacy of the process, and the accessibility of tools and materials. There was no tedious warping-up of looms or hand-spinning of yarn, and if I was less than satisfied with a particular area, it could be undone and recreated very simply.

03

03 NanC Meinhardt, *Hatching Rocks*, *2009. 25 x 36 cm (10 x 14 in). Embroidered, free-form right-angle weave; glass seed beads.*

Acquiring the necessary tools for this craft involves little expense. Rummaging around thrift stores and charity shops for fabrics is most definitely part of the preliminary fun. The basic methods and techniques of rag-rugging are easily learned, and somehow with their repetitive motions are soothing and relaxing too. There is certainly scope for making a broad range of both decorative and functional items: cushions and corsages, hangings and handbags. The possibilities for collaborative making, as a family, a group of friends, or a school or community project, are diverse. In my many projects over the years, with different groups, young and old, it is obvious to me that rag-rugging, rather like the traditional quilting bee, is socially as well as creatively therapeutic,

04 *Well-dressing, Eyam, Derbyshire.*

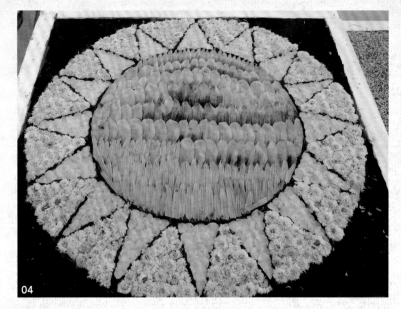

05 **El Anatsui,** *DZESI II, 2006. 303 x 463 cm (121 in x 185 in). Aluminium bottle caps, copper wire.*

9

offering the opportunity to participate on so many levels. This might simply involve contributions of cast-off clothing, or the provision of anecdotal information to inform the design of a wall hanging. As well as being enjoyed by children, it can be a beautiful translator of their artwork; and part of its appeal for an older generation undoubtedly lies in the memories triggered. Aesthetically, the medium often seems to be enriched by its collaborative nature.

The density and compactness of the looped or tufted pile produce a sturdy and durable finished textile, and as long as this is not exposed constantly to harsh sunlight, the colours retain their vibrancy. I have been told many stories of stair runners made during the 1930s and earlier, which are still well and truly intact despite having been subjected to phenomenal wear and tear.

The terminology attached to the tools and methods of rug-making are, to some extent, geographically dependent. In County Durham, for instance, the word 'proggie' would replace 'probby', used in Berwick-upon-Tweed, or 'peggy' and 'tabby' in other regions. All indicate the method of pushing short strips of mostly recycled fabric through the reverse of a hessian backing cloth, to achieve a soft, thick, shaggy pile. Hooking and prodding involve the use of different tools, and achieve different surfaces. As basic textile processes, however, they combine and are compatible with other materials and ways of working. Some of my projects will, I hope, encourage you to explore these possibilities.

06 **Lynne Stein with Simonstone Primary School and Eleanor Palmer** (detail). *Gawthorpe Hall residency, 2000.*

07 **Las Rancheritas Rug Hook Project,** *Oralia Mermaid, 2010. 92 x 81 cm (36 x 32 in). Hooked wool and polar fleece. Picture: Charlotte Bell.*

08 **Copyright Heather Ritchie/RugAid,** *2009. An ongoing project involving people with visual impairment.*

Rag rugs were born out of necessity, as a way of adding some domestic warmth to an otherwise cold stone floor. Increased ecological awareness, the fashion for wooden and stone floors to replace wall-to-wall carpets, and a certain revived interest in 'home crafts' and domesticity, indicated by the advent of stitch 'n' bitch groups, cupcakes and crochet, all contribute to the resurgence in the relevance and popularity of rag rugs within the lands of their origins and beyond. Guilds and groups continue to thrive on both sides of the Atlantic, museums and galleries exhibit and introduce the work of both established and less well-known makers, and magazines, newsletters, blogs and forums are published, always with something new to say.

Socially and economically beneficial projects and inspiring innovations are being run in various parts of the world, from Heather Ritchie's Rug Aid in the Gambia, Mielie in South Africa, and Las Rancheritas in Mexico, to the wonderful hooked woollen textiles made by adults with developmental disabilities, at the Creative Growth Art Centre in California. The rugs made by Moroccan Berber women are known as Boucherouite rugs, from the Moroccan-Arabic term *bu sherwit*, meaning 'a piece torn from used clothing'. It would be hard to surpass these as a stunning example of the links between necessity and inventiveness. Synthetic fibres, including lurex, nylon and plastic, now provide the weft materials, and the means of continuing a tradition and livelihood from rug-making, since widespread drought in the 1980s caused a devastating scarcity of wool.

09 **Ronald Veasey, Creative Growth Arts Centre, Bar-B-Que,** *1990. 90 x 106 cm (35 x 42 in). Hooked wool.*

10 **Boucherouite rug,** *late 20th century. 122 x 127 cm (48 x 50 in). Knotted with a symmetrical knot pile. Rag and lurex. Picture: Gebhart Blazek / courtesy berber-arts.com*

09

10

11 **Ali Rhind,** *Totems, 1996 (part of a larger installation). Prodded wool. Photograph by David Lawson.*

Rag-rugging as a medium frequently appeals to painters, stitchers, graphic artists and sculptors alike, for its versatility and its capacity for enhancing creativity, renewing colour theories, and exploring textile behaviours. It is an addictive craft! It is my hope that this book will introduce new ideas, techniques and ways of working; also that it will also demonstrate the application of rag-rugging for and within a diverse range of settings, including schools, libraries, hospitals and residential homes for the elderly.

History

The technique of constructing a textile by manipulating loops or tufts through a woven foundation is a very old one; it probably precedes the technique of knotted pile, dating back to ancient Coptic textiles, around 2000 BC, in Egypt. The first examples of rugs were evident in Danish Bronze Age graves, and somewhat later in Viking and Celtic tombs. Ann Macbeth, Head of Embroidery at Glasgow School of Art from 1911 until 1920, wrote that the methods were introduced to the Scots by the Vikings. Their construction was of raw fleece loops, which emulated the feel and warmth of sheepskin, and would have been used mostly for bed coverings, replacing the earlier skins and furs. The Shetland Isles were part of Norway until the fifteenth century, and similar textile methods were evident here until this time.

Rugs made from fabric remnants are in fact common to several cultures, and their forerunners and influences, in terms of looped pile, include ropework and the textile traditions of sailors and their wives, medieval tambour work, and possibly the Spanish Alpujarra peasant rugs, from the fifteenth to the nineteenth century.

The oldest surviving rag rug in Britain apparently used army uniforms worn in the Battle of Waterloo in 1815. The heyday of rag-rug making in the UK, however, was the late nineteenth and early twentieth centuries. Beyond the Industrial Revolution, the availability of cheap mass-produced fabrics and clothing, access to mill remnants and thrums for 'rags', and the advent of jute hessian from India in the 1850s, were certainly contributing factors to continued practice of the craft. Sacks which had contained flour, sugar, potatoes and coffee were also imported from India, and could occasionally be coaxed from a friendly grocer. From the early twentieth century, hessian or burlap could be purchased quite cheaply by the yard, and ready-printed designs had also become more affordable.

12 Unknown maker, *Tiger Rug*, 1960s.
106 x 76 cm (42 x 30 in). Bewcastle area.
Picture: Maureen Morano.

The reason for the relative lack of documentation of rag-rug making in the British Isles is partly due to the fact that, in its day, it was undervalued as a craft. There is a scarcity of examples in museum collections, because most rugs were worn through before making it that far. Often having been worked in the autumn months to brighten the Christmas hearth, they would gradually, during the course of the year, be demoted, via the scullery, eventually reaching the privy or the compost heap outside!

It is easy to romanticise the craft as practised then, and to forget the blistered fingers, the cutting-out of seams and other preparatory tasks, not to mention the sheer weight of the work as it progressed. The origins of rag-rug making were probably European, but in Britain, unlike North America and Scandinavia, it was simply a folk art born of necessity and rooted in poverty, and as much an activity of everyday life as brewing tea and darning socks.

The craft could involve the whole family, demanding only minimal skills and negligible cost. The men would often draw the design of a rug with a fire-charred stick, and usually made the rug frames, which were sometimes shared amongst an entire street. Frames were used, especially in Scotland and northern England, to speed up the work; they would be the focal point of the living room, occupying most of the available space and most of the family's attention! Tools might be fashioned from nails, keys, whale bones, sheep's horn and carved parasol handles.

Sometimes they were made at the local blacksmith, foundry or shipyard. In the 1920s and 1930s, family cohesion was expressed in the making of a 'clippie' mat to adorn the hearth, which took pride of place in the home. Children were often only allowed out to play once their quota of 'hookie' or 'proggie' pieces had been cut!

13 **Unknown maker,** *1930s–40s. 145 x 77 cm (57 x 30 in). Picture. Maureen Morano.*

14 **Unknown maker,** *19th century. Recycled soft-furnishing scraps, black wool on hessian. A common motif within the rugs of fishing communities, the diamond was believed to avert the evil eye. Picture: Scottish Fisheries Museum. Donated by Mrs Doig, Cellardyke, 1970s. Photograph by Vicky Brown.*

There is a strong history of making rag rugs from Motherwell to Morecambe Bay, and particularly in Tyneside, but there is evidence of the craft in most parts of the UK, especially in mining, seafaring and rural farming communities. The only real differences are the local terms for tools and techniques, such as 'tabbie', 'proggie' and 'bodger'. Methods and traditions only differed slightly according to region and circumstances, such as the use, in fishing communities, of trawlermens' jersey wool for the 'rags', and kipper dyes to produce beautiful shades of brown and orange. Since the usual source of material for a rug was a worn-out tweed jacket or a pair of old woollen breeches (no item of family clothing being discarded), colours were often earthy and sombre. Red material, occasionally salvaged from a flannel petticoat or a military uniform, was often coveted and considered to have protective powers, and used 'to ward away the devil, should he look down the chimney'.

In mining families particularly, bed coverings made for the winter were later used as 'summer mats', while in many fishing communities, everyday mats were removed to make room for the Sunday mat. In some areas, the tradition of 'rolling in the new mat' was a ritualised celebration, undertaken by the youngest child of the household.

Although there was a lull in making after the First World War, rag rugs were made well into the 1930s, particularly in more economically depressed areas. By the Second World War, with its 'make-do-and-mend' imperative, the availability of synthetic dyes and different materials had increased, and other methods and techniques such as dyeing, knitting and crochet were occasionally incorporated into rugs.

The prodded or pegged rug was common in the north east and the south of England, creating simple but utilitarian rugs for warmth. These were also made in Scotland and the north west: 'hookies' and 'clippies' (terms to distinguish between looped and tufted rug piles) were popular, the loops sometimes being sheared to give a softer, even texture. Until the 1960s, patterns were generally simple, often using household crockery, brown paper or cardboard cutouts as templates for geometric motifs or scalloped borders. Cumbrian rugs often featured a central lozenge shape, surrounded by an area of random mixed colours, known as 'mizzy-mazzy', and dark borders, which were frequently made from stockings. The designs of this region gradually became more figurative and pictorial, often featuring animals such as cows, bulls and horses. 'Crazy paving' designs influenced by patchwork quilts were also popular. For several decades after the war, the craft virtually disappeared, due to negative associations with poverty, and affordable options for floor coverings, including wall-to-wall carpet.

15 **Elizabeth Nunn,** *Sydney, Australia, circa 1939. Dyed woollen fabric scraps tufted onto a knitted string and hessian base. The maker moved to Australia from Britain in 1901, and worked as a corsetiere in a large Sydney department store, where many of the rug's offcuts were obtained. Donated by and copyright Grace Flinn. Collection: Powerhouse Museum, Sydney. Photograph by Jean-François Lazarone.*

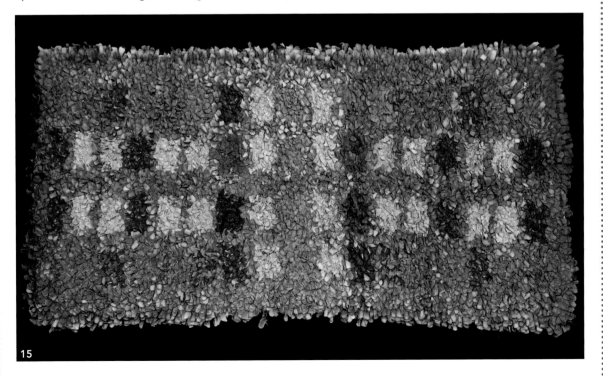

15

16 Margaret Warwick, *Two Cats by the Fire, circa 1923. 58 x 124 cm (23 x 49 in). Margaret Warwick was Winifred Nicholson's next-door neighbour, and the work features in one of Ben Nicholson's drawings from this era. Picture: Tullie House Museum and Art Gallery Trust. Photograph by Guy Paule.*

17 Hooked by Florence Williams, *1960s. The tweeds in the border, which so distinguish her work, were obtained from Otterburn Mill, where she was employed. Picture: Maureen Morano.*

18

In the early 1920s, soon after they were married, the artists Winifred and Ben Nicholson settled in Cumberland, close to Winifred's childhood home, and were impressed by the charming and primitive designs of rag rugs made by their neighbours. Among them, Margaret Warwick and her daughters, Janet Heap and Mary Bewick, created rugs which were regarded as 'folk art' and attracted collectors. In the 1960s, after divorcing, Winifred, on whom the resourcefulness of the Cumbrian lifestyle had left an enduring impression, was approached by Nancy Powell, another enthusiastic craftsperson, to engender local interest in the craft. With the help of her son Jake, and her grandchildren, approximately one hundred and eighty rugs were designed. Many of these were made by Mrs Davidson from Bewcastle and Florence Williams. Living next door to Otterburn Mill at Warwick Bridge, a popular source for fabric offcuts, Miss Williams, noted for her vibrant palette, would often search through mill clippings to obtain just the right colours for the rugs.

In the 1970s, in nearby Lanercost, artists Audrey and Denis Barker, with the intention of improving design standards, involved local makers such as Florence Williams in the execution and interpretation of their designs. Like Winifred Nicholson, they encouraged all makers to express their individuality in terms of colour and occasional compositional adjustments.

19 **Unknown maker**, *mid-20th century. 120 x 86 cm (47 x 34 in). Picture: Maureen Morano.*

Crafts such as rug-making, patchwork and quilting were taken by emigrants to North America, initially to maritime areas such as Maine, New England, New Brunswick, Nova Scotia, Prince Edward Island, Quebec, Newfoundland and Labrador. By the end of the nineteenth century, rugs were made all over North America.

Fishing and farming were common ways of life during this time, and families faced harsh and austere conditions and severe, lengthy winters. Thrift and resourcefulness were essential in furnishing their humble homes. Given that all the preliminary processes for clothing the family and furnishing the home, such as weaving, spinning and dyeing, were hugely labour-intensive, every scrap of fabric was cherished and eventually transformed into a patchwork quilt or a hooked rug. These textile crafts provided a vehicle for creativity, introducing warmth and cheer into an otherwise dismal and unwelcoming domestic environment.

Imported carpets, and even those which were factory-made by the 1820s, were prohibitively expensive. Floor coverings had often consisted merely of grease-absorbing sand, swept into swirls, chevron and herringbone patterns. Amongst wealthier families, floors were also decorated with stencilling and painted floorcloths. Until the 1830s, the earliest 'ruggs' or 'ryiiys', with their long Scandinavian history, were actually bed coverings, and add meaning to the saying 'snug as a bug in a rug'! By the mid-nineteenth century, imported Indian jute hessian, known as burlap, provided an efficient and affordable backing cloth. This changed the course of rug-making. Hooking, because of its durability and defined imagery, now superseded such earlier techniques as braiding, shirring, yarn sewing, pulled 'shag mats' and appliquéd 'dollar mats'. Designs for the earliest hooked rugs were drawn freehand and reflected the maker's domestic environment, including farmstead animals, flowers and fruit. Outer edges were often given linear borders or adorned with scallops, scrolls and floral forms. Ships, shells and other depictions of marine life appeared in the rug designs of sailors' wives, and would be surrounded by backgrounds of contrasting colour and texture. Patriotic themes also adorned some rugs, bearing the eagle or American flag, and slogans or words such as 'Union'. During the nineteenth century, the Shakers, who were skilled designers and craftspeople, developed their own style. Their rugs, which could be sold for 70 cents per square foot, display evidence of the importance they placed on function, aesthetics and thrift.

By the end of the nineteenth century, cheaper carpets became available, and home rug-making declined. However, as in Britain, the American Arts and Crafts movement grew out of a dissatisfaction with mass production, and a desire to preserve traditional skills. Design ideas came from numerous sources, including geometric shapes, overlapping

20 *Unknown maker, General George Washington,* circa 1880. 145 x 102 cm (57 x 40 in). Hooked wool and wool jersey. Political and patriotic themes feature frequently in American hooked rugs of the period. Picture: Just Folk, California.

clamshells, traditional patchwork quilts or more elaborate carpet patterns in catalogues. Animals on metal weathervanes, as well as stencils and domestic crockery, were used as templates, and paintings and furniture carvings were copied. Narrative scenes recorded family events, and were occasionally accompanied by humorous phrases or wise sayings. As in Britain, one of the simplest but most effective designs was a mixture of multi-coloured fabrics in a random manner, known in America as 'hit or miss'. Until the 1860s, when chemical dyes became available (some seven hundred by 1902), a wide but subtle colour palette could be obtained from leaves, berries, plants and vegetables, such as brazilwood, walnut, hickory, sumac, elderberry, cochineal and onion skins. Rugs with a relief surface from sculpted pile, perhaps depicting a floral wreath, an animal or a basket of fruit, became known as Waldoboro rugs, from the town of their origin in Maine.

Attempts were being made to make the craft of rug-making more accessible. The first printed rug designs appeared in the 1850s. In the 1860s, Edward Sands Frost, a tinware pedlar from Maine, observed his wife's rug hooking attempts with poor tools and designs, and set about creating stencils for printing, made from old copper boilers. In 1881 Ebenezer Ross patented the Novelty Rug Machine, which, resembling a shuttle hook, helped to speed up the hooking process. Towards the end of the century, mail-order firms such as Sears Roebuck and Montgomery Ward featured patterns for printed designs in their catalogues, many of which were copies of both Frost and Ross. While it could be said that a 'painting by numbers' approach might have stifled creativity, it certainly popularised the craft, and many makers adapted the designs and introduced colourways according to their own taste. Helen Rickey Albee was one of the first during the Arts and Crafts movement to set up a cottage industry in New Hampshire, outsourcing work to the local farmers' wives. In the early part of the twentieth century, several other cottage industries followed, many designs being inspired by Native American designs, and all enabling the rug-makers to earn extra income.

With the Colonial Revival style, interest in early American crafts increased. During the Arts and Crafts Movement, exhibitions showcasing the rugs were more frequent, and provided continuing sales outlets for cottage industries such as the Subbekashe Rug Industry, at the beginning of the twentieth century. Country folk erected stalls along the roadside or sold their work from home.

From the 1920s, with increasing mobility and car ownership, collectors and interior decorators would travel considerable distances to New England and Canada in search of an 'antique': a rare hooked rug, displaying all the patience, skill, and often humour, of its maker. During the 1940s, auction sales of rugs took place, particularly in New York.

In 1892, William Grenfell, an English doctor, was sent as a missionary to deep-sea fishermen on the Canadian coast of Labrador. Although he found appalling conditions – extreme poverty, lack of hygiene and consequent sickness – he was charmed by both the place and the people, and decided the following year to dedicate his life to improving theirs, by setting up the Grenfell Mission. Hospitals, schools and industries were established, as was the Mission boat offering mobile medical help.

Although early French influence is apparent, Grenfell regarded the tradition of rug-hooking as having probably been brought to the Canadian maritime provinces by Scottish and Cornish settlers who had learnt the craft as children. Although the local women were obviously familiar with the techniques and had great expertise in making, they mainly used dowdy old clothes for fabrics, and he was disappointed by the lack of design and colour sense in their work. Acknowledging rug-making as a viable means of earning money, and the necessity of raising standards to meet the requirements of wealthy collectors in the US and Canada, he engaged Miss Jesse Luther, an occupational therapist and talented designer, to supervise the work of up to two thousand women per year. Designs were often figurative, displaying local animals such as reindeer and beavers, and maritime themes.

21 **Grenfell mat,** *circa 1970s. 41 x 30 cm (16 x 12 in). Finely hooked wool on hessian. Picture: Anne and Malvin Flynn.*

21

22

Later Rhoda Dawson, whose designs were rather more modern and abstract, took over. In the 1930s and 40s, responding to the slogan, 'when your stocking starts to run, let it run to Labrador', supporters of the Mission sent silk and rayon stockings to replace the flannelette which had been formerly used for the mats. Sales outlets were established in Canada, along the eastern seaboard, Philadelphia, Vermont and as far away as England.

As demand from collectors in America continued to grow, original designs were still being executed well into the twentieth century. At the end of the nineteenth century, on Cape Breton Island, Nova Scotia, an artist by the name of Lillian Burke was engaged by the wife of Alexander Graham Bell to set up the Cheticamp Hooked Rug Industry. Again, she noted the obvious potential amongst local makers, but was unimpressed by their choice of colours and pledged to improve design standards. Demand occasionally called for large-scale rugs, with several women working together on one piece for months at a time. Design inspiration occasionally came from museum collections of paintings and textiles. Earnings from rug-making sometimes constituted a family's entire income.

Very much a winter occupation, when fishing and farming were less busy, rug-making was equally well established in Newfoundland and Nova Scotia, and there are similarities between these and the rugs from New

22 **Elizabeth le Fort,** *Crucifixion, 1964. 168 x 300 cm (66 x 120 in). Including five hundred and ten hand-dyed colours, this painterly work took one hundred and eighty-seven days to hook! Picture: Les Trois Pignons, Cheticamp.*

England, although the Americans normally used pure wool rather than a mixture of materials. The earlier examples, made by French settlers in Nova Scotia and Cape Breton Island, were sheared yarn-sewn rugs, creating an undulating, sculptural pile, distinguishing the central motif from its background and bearing some resemblance to the Waldoboro rugs. The craft was also evident in Quebec and Ontario, where the tradition seems to have survived for centuries, with influences including tambour and ecclesiastical embroidery. By 1900, 'stamped mats' were available here. Designs were also stabbed with a needle, through the outline of a shape onto thick brown paper, to be cut into a template.

Debate about the origins of rag rugs, both geographically and chronologically, continues. It is clear that as well as having been a thrift craft, at times it has also afforded makers the opportunity of creating powerful and personal visual statements. Like previous cottage industries on both sides of the Atlantic, relatively new initiatives, which also aim to empower and improve the lives of rug-makers and their families, emerge continually in different parts of the world. Today, rag rugs, as well as carrying the creative expression of the maker, resonate with current ecological concerns, and the desire once more to conserve, recycle and repurpose.

23 Mielie, *hooked t-shirt fabrics. Mielie is a business initiative in Capetown, creating bags and homeware products. Masterminded by Adri Schutz, it provides employment for about fifty women, allowing them to work from home.*

24

Materials, tools and equipment

3

One of the advantages of this craft is that it is not expensive to get started. As a beginner, you need only very basic equipment: a simple frame, backing cloth, scissors, a rug hook and a range of materials.

Materials

Your choice of fabrics will very much depend on your project. If you are planning a rug or mat for the floor, you will need to consider such factors as shrink and dye resistance, washability and general durability. Certain synthetic fibres are extremely hardwearing. However, if you are aiming for something more decorative and pictorial, such as a wall hanging or even a cushion, the possibilities are almost limitless.

Medium-weight woollen fabrics and flannels can be suitable and will take dyes well, but they are also relatively expensive. Car-boot sales, charity shops, cast-offs and occasionally fabric websites, can all provide rewarding and inexpensive sources for developing your range of colours, weights and textures. Scarves, shawls and wraps, as well as certain larger items of clothing, can prove to be excellent finds. Keepsake and 'rite of passage' garments such as ties, wedding dresses and christening robes might make a very personal heirloom piece.

As well as judging a fabric on its suitability for the job, you should take its aesthetic appearance into consideration. Available fabrics might include crimplene, velour, organza, net, satin, silk, polyester, towelling, plastic, paper, ribbon, lurex, nylon, soft and supple leather and suede, sweet wrappers, cotton, wool, lace, fleece, knitwear and linen. As well as dyed and natural unspun merino fleece, a wide range of yarns can also be introduced, such as mohair, rug and knitting wool, chenille, embroidery and sari silk, linen and metallic thread, slub, space-dyed and novelty yarns.

24 A selection of fabrics, fibres, scoobies, ribbons, braids and other embellishment artefacts.

When trying to estimate the amount of fabric required for your strips, roughly fold the fabric in four over the area of the design to be worked. However, I personally find that running out of a certain fabric is rarely a disaster, as part of the medium's charm and richness is the blending of closely related tones and textures.

Dyeing fabrics for a particular project is less common in the UK, where there seems to be less concern for intricate tonal gradations and hyperrealism.

All fabrics should be washed before use, and any buttons, pockets, waistbands, collars, cuffs, zips and facings removed. However, like torn or frayed edges, stitched and overlocked fabrics can provide textural interest in your work. You will find it helpful eventually to sort your fabrics into colours and store them in transparent plastic bags or stacking boxes.

Backing cloths

The prime considerations for selecting the appropriate backing cloth or foundation fabric are that the weave should be sufficiently open and even, and easy to manipulate with your tools. The fabric should be non-stretch, stable and durable. This might include linen, monk's cloth, wide-mesh rug canvas and even certain plastic garden meshes, in the case of an exterior project. However, you might also wish to try using knitted or crocheted fabrics, which can result in quite a warm and substantial fabric.

Rug canvas is likely to dictate a somewhat more linear and geometric approach. Traditionally, the backing cloth for a rug would have been hessian or burlap. This is still commonly used, and generally should be bought as best quality 280g (10 oz) weight or finer, depending on the project. It is normally sold in 90 and 120 cm (3 and 4 ft) widths. If using recycled sacks, it is important that there are no holes or flaws in the weave, which could spoil your work.

Frames

A frame will achieve and maintain tautness in your backing cloth, making hooking far easier. It must allow for periodic viewing of the textile you're working on, and its size must allow you to reach the

25

25 *The author at work in her studio.*

centre of your work easily. To begin with, you may just use a simple, inexpensive, wooden canvas stretcher. These are available in various sizes, and your work can be moved along the frame as a section is completed. As you progress, you may find it handy to have a variety of frames in different shapes and sizes.

Quilting hoops, particularly when working with fine yarns and thinly cut strips of material, can be ideal for jewellery and small projects. Square pine frames can be quickly assembled and taken apart, and can be either propped up against a table or chair back. There are a variety of lap and floor frames, and combinations of both, which use carding strips or gripper rods along each side to secure the backing cloth. These have the advantage of freeing your hands, and will swivel and rotate for ease. An adjustable rolling frame can be particularly useful if embarking on a sizeable piece of work or a collaborative project. This is comparable to a traditional rug or quilting frame, with carpet webbing tacked along the two long sides, onto which the backing cloth can be stitched. Two movable slats slide through these bars, with pegs for tensioning, and can be released and reassembled to expose the next part of the design. The frame can be set up on trestles or table tops of the same height.

Hooks

The specific function of the type of hook you choose will be important, as will its size and feel for comfort. A smooth, turned yew rug hook handle, for instance, can be very comforting and therapeutic to use. With luck, old rug hooks can occasionally be found in junk shops or on websites.

The standard 'primitive' rug hook is appropriate for executing the majority of the projects in this book. You may also find an extra-fine pencil hook useful for working with yarns and very fine fabric strips on smaller scale projects.

Spring-clip hooks or bodgers can be used without a frame, and create a thick shaggy surface, comparable to pegged or prodded rugs.

Speed hooks, shuttle hooks and punch needles can be useful and speedy tools, creating a 'walking' motion across the reverse side of the backing cloth, to produce a row of loops on the other side. Their slight limitations might include having less flexibility with the width of your rag strip, and the need to constantly review your work on the opposite or right side.

Latch hooks are not entirely appropriate, as they create a knotted pile but no actual knotting is necessary for rag-rugging. This tool is more suited to working on rug canvas, making a thicker pile.

The locker needle combines a wide eye at one end and a hook at the other. It pulls yarn through the loops created, and provides an extra secure surface, holding the loops fast and giving a slightly woven appearance. Different sizes are available for different scales of work.

Prodders

Historically, these were fashioned from any number of available items, from parasol handles to clothes pegs and whale bones, the crucial factor being the smooth point, made for pushing the fabric through a space in the backing cloth. Once again, a smooth, bulbous-handled prodder can make for more comfort, and various types are available, made from both wood and metal.

Dolly pegs, with one side sawn off and the other carved to a smooth point, can also be used. Even pencils or crayons can be used when working with a class of young children.

26

26 A varied collection of prodders. Picture: Ali Rhind. Photograph by Jane Frazer.

Cutting tools

Generally my preference is simply for a range of scissors of different sizes. I use long-bladed shears, embroidery scissors, napping shears with offset handles, and sharp scissors with shorter blades for trimming off stray ends of threads and fabric, and for fine detailed work, such as fleece and yarn sculpting. Pinking shears can be useful for cutting pieces of fabric for prodding, particularly with sturdy materials like felt, and for creating extra texture. Many fabrics such as cotton and polyester can be snipped and torn along their grain, sometimes producing an attractive frayed edge.

You may find a rotary cutter and cutting board helpful, as these will help to produce straight and even strips of fabric.

A machine cutter, which can be clamped onto a table, can also be a useful piece of equipment. However, these are quite expensive and are more easily available in the US. They do not handle synthetic or flimsy fabrics, such as crimplene and nylon, well, and although they allow different cutting widths, changing the blades to achieve this is time consuming.

Other useful equipment

- Sewing machine, needles, pins, bodkins, kilt and safety pins, string, threads
- Iron and pressing cloth, old towels
- Drawing pins, hammer, staple gun and staples, staple remover
- Compasses, stiff card or cereal boxes for templates
- Masking tape

- Graph paper, tracing paper, non-stick baking parchment, carbon paper, brown paper, drawing paper, clear acetate
- Indelible thick and thin marker pens, tailor's chalk, transfer pencil
- Ruler, metal yardstick, tape measure
- Pair of trestles, G-clamps
- Heat gun

- Latex carpet adhesive, metal or plastic spreader, all-purpose glue
- Crochet hook, knitting needles, felting needles, felting mat or sponge
- Flexible wire, scoobies
- Beads, buttons, glass nuggets, pompoms, shisha mirrors, junk jewellery, etc.

A sewing machine might come in handy for sewing hems, attaching linings, and joining rag-rug panels. A variety of needles are useful for various tasks, from stitching with rag strips, to attaching hessian onto the webbing of a rug frame. If you are doing any plaiting or braiding, you will need large kilt pins to anchor your fabric as you work.

An iron will be useful for transferring designs onto your hessian, and also for heat-bonding processes, for which you will also need towels and non-stick baking parchment. Acetate sheets, rulers and yardsticks can also be useful aids for scaling and transferring designs. Tailor's chalk is helpful, particularly if you are a little nervous about drawing, to mark the preliminary stages of your design before making the final draft with coloured markers.

If you are using trestles, G-clamps will help to secure your rug frame. Masking tape can be used to protect hessian or tapestry canvas edges from fraying, as well as for sticking drawings and tracings to the hessian when transferring your design.

Latex adhesive, rather than PVA, may be spread onto the back of a rug as a final process. This will prevent any fabrics from being dislodged, provide a non-slip surface – if the rug is to be placed on a hard floor – and make it easy to roll (rather than fold) if necessary. The same adhesive, generally available from hardware stores, is used for fixing carpet tiles. It is best to apply this with a card, plastic or metal spreader in a well-ventilated area.

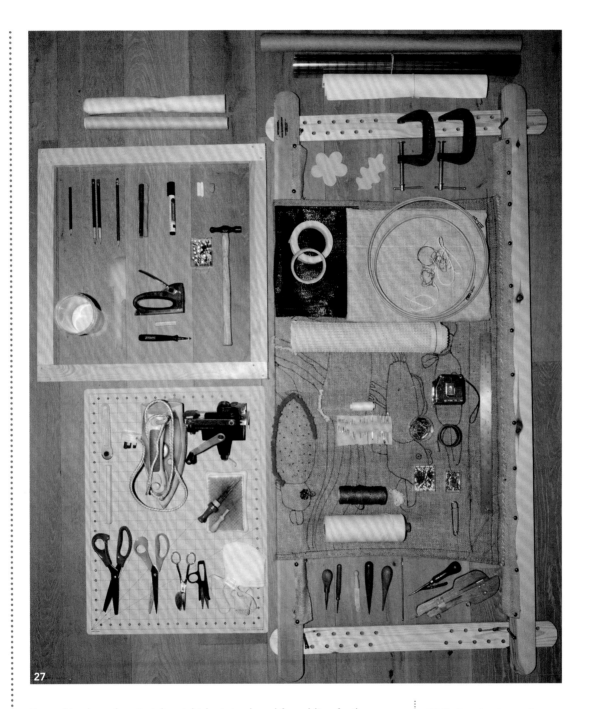

27

Several tools and materials might be introduced for adding further decorative embellishment and interesting surfaces to your work, from a heat gun to felting equipment, and buttons, beads and discarded junk jewellery, which can be stuck or stitched into your work.

27 *Tools and equipment for a range of projects of different sizes and techniques.*

Making processes

4

Preparation

Cutting strips

It is sometimes difficult to establish precisely the amount of material needed for different areas of your design, and you may find it helpful to create a sample of that area first. The width of your fabric strip will depend upon its weight and quality, your chosen technique, and the desired effect. For prodding, the average size of your pieces should be 7.5 x 2 cm (3 x ¾ in). The pieces can be cut in different ways, leaving straight, angled or pinked ends, which will affect the texture of your work.

28

28 *Cutting pieces of fabric for prodding.*

A fabric gauge can be a useful tool, as it enables you to cut short, uniform strips, perfect for prodding. For hooking, you will need long strips, the width ranging from approximately 1–2.5 cm (⅓–1 in), depending on the fabric. For example, a soft nylon or polyester fabric would be cut into wider strips than thick, woollen sweater fabric. Generally the thicker the fabric, the denser the appearance will be. A rotary cutter and mat can help in ensuring consistent strip widths. Certain garments, and fabrics like felt, can be folded first, allowing you to speed up the process by cutting through several layers simultaneously. Many fabrics, including cottons and organza, will tear well along the grain. A more frayed edge will be apparent, but combined with smoother non-fraying fabrics, interesting and attractive textural contrast can be achieved in your work. To obtain a long continuous length, make a small cut at the beginning of each length, repeating this process as you turn your fabric around to cut and tear it in the opposite direction. You will have angled corners on the fabric, but these can eventually be trimmed or will be hidden within your hooking.

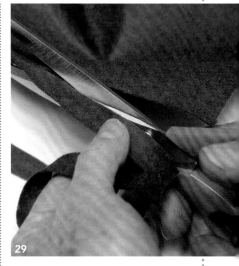

29 *Cutting a continuous length of fabric for hooking.*

Stretching backing cloth

Most hooked work requires the use of some kind of frame, depending on the size of your project. To aid ease of hooking and minimise physical strain, the backing cloth should be stretched as taut as possible when attaching it to the frame. To achieve straight and parallel edges, and for measurement accuracy, pull a thread from the hessian to give you a straight line. If you are using a square mat-making frame or stretcher, place the frame over the centre of your backing cloth, ensuring warp and weft are straight, to avoid eventual distortion of your design. You should then have a sufficient excess of cloth to fold around each side of the frame, which will also create further tension once pinned or stapled. Start attaching the cloth along one side, at 5 cm (2 in) intervals, leaving the corners loose. Pulling the cloth taut, work the opposite side. Repeat this process on the remaining two sides, neatly folding in all excess backing cloth, and finally folding in the corners so that they have a mitred appearance.

30 *Stretching and attaching the backing cloth to the frame with a staple gun, showing a mitred corner.*

If you are using a large adjustable rug frame, the hemmed design on your backing cloth should be placed centrally and stitched with strong linen thread to the lengths of webbing on each long side of your frame. The width of your work will be determined by the length of your webbing, but since the backing is rolled around the rug frame as the work progresses, its length is limitless.

Transferring designs

When transferring your design, bear in mind that if it is going to be worked in the prodded method, it should be drafted onto the reverse side of your backing cloth, which, since done from back to front, will be facing you as you proceed. Otherwise, in most cases, the design would be drafted directly onto the right side of the cloth. Whether the design is drafted before or after stretching the cloth on a frame, take care not to distort the design.

If freehand drawing does not come easily to you, there are several options for transferring an entire design onto your backing cloth. The use of a photocopier or a scanner and printer for the purposes of enlarging or reducing a design, can be invaluable. It might be necessary to repeat this process several times, turning the image to fit, to achieve the required size.

You can make stiff card templates of the overall and basic shapes in your design. Draw around these, first with tailor's chalk and then with an indelible marker, which should be broad tipped to cope with the coarseness of hessian.

A transfer pencil or tracing wheel, tracing paper and an iron can be used. Having traced your design with the transfer pencil, pin the drawn side of the paper facing the backing cloth and press with a hot, dry iron. To avoid overheating either surface, rather than gliding the iron, move it systematically across the design, with vertical movements, ensuring all areas are subjected to heat. Bear in mind that the transferred design will be the reverse of the original.

Alternatively, a darning needle can be used to prick holes along the design's outlines. Once the punctured tracing paper is positioned on the backing cloth, pounce or powdered tailor's chalk should be sprinkled over the drawn area, its penetration through the holes being aided by a soft-bristle toothbrush. The outlines can then be redefined with a permanent marker. Similarly, if the design is drawn onto tissue paper and pinned to the backing cloth, small running stitches should be sewn along the outlines of the design. The tissue paper can then be carefully separated from the stitched backing cloth, and the outlines clarified with a marker pen.

Your original design can be overlaid with an acetate sheet grid, the equal grid squares becoming a guide for making it larger or smaller. The

31

31 *Card templates, grid marked hessian and corresponding acetate grid overlay on the rug design.*

more detailed your design, the smaller the grid squares should be. The same even grid should be drawn on your backing cloth, with the scale adjusted as required. Working square by square, copy the markings from the original grid to the backing cloth, until the designs match. You could use tailor's chalk initially, and then permanent marker once you are satisfied with the result.

Dressmaker's or artist's carbon paper is useful too. Placing the ink side facing the cloth, pin your design over the carbon paper and draw firmly over the outlines with a dressmaker's pencil until the markings are transferred.

A lightbox can be improvised by taping your heavily outlined design on thin paper to a clear glass window and placing the fabric over the design. The natural light should reveal the design clearly, enabling it to be traced.

Strong, sheer fabric such as tulle can be used as a transfer fabric. Once bearing the traced design, this should be positioned securely on your backing cloth, the outlines being traced with a permanent marker, ensuring that they seep through to the cloth.

Techniques

The techniques described below can be used separately, or can be combined to produce richer and more textured, decorative surfaces. The type of project will usually dictate the technique and the fabrics you select. For example, if you want to create a soft, warm rug of subtle-toned, abstract design, you might choose to work this entirely by prodding, using dyed, recycled woollen fabrics. By contrast, a decorative wall hanging might combine several techniques and methods of embellishment with a broad palette and range of fabrics and fibres.

Hooking

It is important to be comfortable when hooking, and positioning your frame at an angle to suit you is crucial. Remember to reposition your work as it progresses if using a large rug frame; also remember that you have the option of working from either side, rather than over-stretching and hurting your back. Getting up from your work every half hour or so and having a good stretch is vital.

Working with the right side of the design facing you, the hook should be held like a pencil, with the hand you would normally use. If right-handed, you will find it far easier to work from right to left, and vice versa if you're left-handed. Poking downwards through the backing cloth to open up a space in the weave, your hook, facing the direction of hooking, should be ready to catch your long fabric strip beneath, which is held between the thumb and forefinger of your other hand. This position of the hand will constantly feed the fabric onto the base of the hook. The end of the strip should be pulled through to start the row of loops, leaving a first tuft of approximately 1 cm (½ in) on the top surface.

Continue this motion, next pulling a slightly shorter loop up above the surface of the backing cloth. As you continue forming a row of loops, try to create a fairly even pile height, and an even space between the loops themselves, with just one or two warp threads of the backing cloth between, depending on the weight and thickness of your fabric. Creating a dense surface pile will prevent the work from dislodging; aesthetically, you will usually want to hide any visible backing cloth with the loops of your design. When finishing a fabric strip, bring the end to the top surface, trimming the beginning and end of your hooking to the height of the loops. The reverse of your work should simply show a flat connected running stitch row.

Your loops should be hooked systematically in rows to prevent unworked areas of the design from being blocked and creating bulkiness on the reverse. However, these 'rows' can be vertical, horizontal, diagonal or swirly, rhythmic lines, the direction of your hooking affecting its textural appearance. This technique is particularly suited to detailed, figurative and pictorial areas, and for creating subtle colour and textural blends. Certain designs may also call for longer or irregular loops in areas of your hooking. You can also experiment with pile height, and with blending different fabrics and yarns.

Prodding

This technique can be done on your lap, without the use of a frame. With the reverse side of the backing cloth facing you, use your prodder to make a hole or space, and push half of your short piece of fabric through the hole, leaving one end underneath and the other on top. With an average space of a few warp threads, push the other end through to the right side, so that a tuft of two ends of fabric will have formed on the right side, and a flat stitch on the reverse. Repeat this process, pushing one end of the next piece of fabric into or close by the space holding the last piece. Your spacing will depend on the thickness and weight of the fabric, and on the desired density of pile. It will take time before the design on the right side becomes apparent, as the technique relies upon the completion of juxtaposed areas to clarify each other's shapes. The tufts can finally be adjusted on the right side, and although this is a basic and simple technique, they can be trimmed, sculpted, stitched, painted and embellished, to create rich surfaces.

32 *Hooking a row of loops along the outline.*

33 *Prodding.*

34 *The prodded surface.*

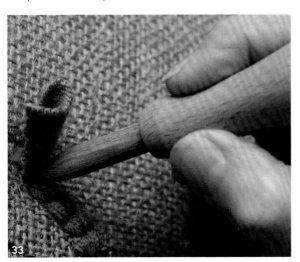

Alternatively, this sort of surface can be worked with a spring-clip tool, sometimes known as a rag-rugger or bodger. In this case, the work is done from the front, pulling each fabric strip through two or three threads in your hessian with the tweezer-like action of the tool. The number of strips pulled through will dictate the density of pile, and you should try to ensure that they are worked closely enough to prevent any exposure of the hessian, or any of the pieces falling out. An average spacing of four or five hessian threads usually works well.

Locker-hooking

Using a wide-mesh rug canvas, 3 to 5 holes per inch, makes a frame unnecessary for this technique because of the canvas's stiffness. Size 5 rug canvas will allow for rather more detail. Hessian can be used as a backing cloth in some cases, for a more free-flowing design. Depending on the desired effect, your long fabric strips should be approximately 1.5–2.5 cm (½–1 in) wide. The edges of your design can be secured either temporarily with masking tape or by mitring the hemmed corners, and using a rug needle and yarn, oversewing these and the folded canvas surplus beyond your design.

Using a 180 cm (6 ft) length of colour-coordinated yarn or cotton twine for the locking medium, thread one end through the eye of your locker hook and tie the other to the starting square of the canvas. Hold the strip of fabric horizontally under the canvas, leaving a 5 cm (2 in) excess. Poke the hook end of the needle through the hole, and pull a 0.5 cm (¼ in) height loop of material through to the top surface of the rug canvas. Keep the loop on your hook and go into the next hole, repeating this process until you have created a row of up to ten loops. Gently pull your threaded locker hook through all the loops, releasing them and ensuring that the locking medium is taut and holds them in place. Continue this process with a new row of loops and the same length of yarn, introducing new material strips and different colours and fabrics as necessary.

35 *Locker hooking.*

Unlike hooking, the ends of the yarn or locking medium should be left on the top surface, whereas the fabric ends should be left underneath to be threaded through loops and trimmed at the end. Combining vertical and horizontal rows, the direction of your hooking will influence the ultimate appearance of your work.

Fleece and yarn sculpting

With effects comparable to the Waldoboro technique (see page 22), this is done in exactly the same way as hooking, but instead of rag strips, teased-out strips of fleece tops or roving are used. Alternatively, you can use several strands of yarn simultaneously, such as carpet wool, mohair or alpaca, or a combination of fleece and yarn. Your loops should be at least 2.5 cm (1 in) in height, and packed extremely closely together. To thicken the pile, you can hook further loops within the work, carefully avoiding creating bulkiness on the reverse. Once the area is sufficiently dense, cut and carve your desired shape with a very sharp pair of scissors. This technique can add a delicious tactile quality to your work, and is useful for creating shapes and areas such as furrowed fields, facial features, motifs and circular shapes.

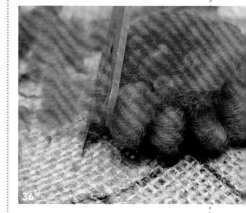

36 *Cutting and sculpting the fleece loops.*

Chain-hooking

The effect achieved here is similar in appearance to embroidered chain stitch, but is thicker and more substantial. You will need a hook and a similar length of rag strip as for hooking. Poke the hook through the backing cloth, and bring the first fabric strip end to the top surface. Insert the hook again, a small distance away, this time pulling a loop through. With the first loop remaining on the hook, and using the same consistent spacing between loops, poke the hook through again, drawing up a second loop. Create the first link by slipping the first loop over the second, gently pulling the stitch flat across the backing cloth's surface. Repeat this motion, forming a chained line. It is worth experimenting with different thicknesses, weights and textures of fabric.

37 *Chain-hooking.*

Wire wrapping

Wrapping a wire with yarn is ideal for creating fluid lines to outline and embellish areas, or to include lettering in your work. Flexible milliner's wire, electrical wire and plastic scoobies are ideal as the core for wrapping. It is advisable to have hooked your preliminary area, on which the wrapping will be attached, first, unless the wrapping itself will form an extra appendage. Establish the approximate length of wire you will need for the shape, and use a liberal length of yarn to wrap. To avoid any unsightly knots on the reverse of your work, thread your wire or scoobie onto a wide-eyed needle and insert it through the top surface of the work, leaving half the total length of wire there. From underneath, in the next space, bring the needle and remaining wire back up to the top, so that you have an anchored double strand of wire on the top to work with. With your chosen thread either single or doubled, start by attaching the yarn to the wire with several lark's head knots (see step f. of the Tote bag project on page 104 for how to do this), and gently push these down to the base of the wire, tightening them. Holding the wire core taut, you can either repeat this process so that the wrapped strand is edged, or for a smooth, tubular appearance, start wrapping the thread around the wire. Periodically push downwards, smoothing it, after wrapping at approximately 1 cm (½ in)intervals, until you have achieved the desired length. Position it into your required shape, then couch it in place, using a length of the same wrapping yarn. Stitch at 0.5 cm (¼ in) intervals over both the wrapped wire and the worked surface underneath. You can vary the width of your wrapping by using different cores and yarns.

38 *Wrapping a scoobie with woollen yarn.*

Needle-felting

Sculptural shapes and relief areas, as well as flat, painterly or graphic surfaces can be achieved with this technique. You will need a felting pad or sponge, woollen fabric or pre-felt, merino fleece tops or roving and assorted woollen yarns. Fibres such as alpaca, angora and llama can also be successfully used. You should have a number of felting needles, as they can tend to break easily. A needle holder is optional. For faster felting and larger areas, holders taking up to four needles are a possibility; however, for shapes within any of my projects, a single needle will suffice. Always work with a sponge or brush mat underneath the work, to support it and absorb the impact of the needle, preventing it from breaking.

Different size or gauge needles produce different effects. The higher the gauge, the more delicate the needle. Fine needles are suited to more decorative, detailed work, while the lower gauge needles are used for forming basic shapes; 36/38 gauge needles will suit most projects.

Because felting needles are barbed, their repetitive stabbing causes the fibres to interlock with one another, creating a more compact woollen fabric. Holding the felting needle, stab it in a straight up-and-down

❯ NOTE
Felting needles are barbed and extremely sharp, so care should be taken not to prick yourself whilst working!

motion through the layers of fabric and fibres, working on a small area at a time, until the layers start to mesh. Working with the needle at an angle can cause it to break. The more you work into an area, the more pronounced your indentations will become. The fibres from the top surface will get partially poked through to the reverse of the cloth. Keep turning the fabric, to prevent it from adhering to the sponge or pad. Work each side until you have achieved the desired effect with tones and textures. You may find that the reverse side becomes the more interesting design with which to continue your felting.

To build up a relief area, use extra fleece, or create several cut shapes of fabric or prefelt, each slightly decreasing in size, and layer these on your base surface before positioning your fleece and fibres over them and starting to needle-felt. A foam core or an armature of pipe cleaners can be used for constructing the base of a three-dimensional form.

Braiding

Braiding can be used as a technique for making rugs on its own, either by coiling or stitching together strips, or you can use it to make borders for other types of rugs.

Taking three strips of fabric approximately 5 cm (2 in) wide, secure the ends with a large safety pin, hooking this over a static object such as a cup hook or coat peg. Roll up each strip of fabric, fastening each end with a pin and gradually release the rolls as you work to avoid them becoming tangled. Begin braiding or plaiting close to the pin, bringing the right strip across the middle one, and then the left strip over the new middle one, trying to achieve a consistent tension and a smooth, flat braid. Try to conceal any raw edges by turning them under towards the reverse or inner side of the braid as you progress. Continue until you have enough strips for your particular project, pinning at the end of each braid length to secure. Remove the pin from the start of the braid, stitch it to conceal any raw edges, and taper this end. Working on a flat surface, coil the braids, which have already been stitched end to end, sewing through the sides of each braid to connect them, for a circular rug. Alternatively, place them alongside one another and stitch through one side of a braid to the next, with a long or curved needle, until all strips are sewn together and a rectangle is formed. To create a border, check that your braid is long enough, and carefully wrap and stitch it around the rug's outer edge. Experiment with different combinations of tones and colourways, as well as fabrics.

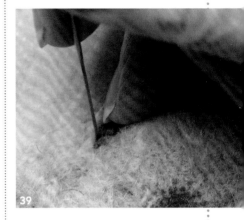

39 Needle-felting.

40 Braiding.

Sampling

It is possible to create interesting marks, textures and surfaces within your work by using and combining hooking and prodding techniques, and different fabrics and yarns. However, particularly for those who are newer to the craft, I like to emphasise the sheer value of 'playing'. You need only be restricted by the limits of your imagination!

Basic hooking and prodding techniques can be combined with knitting, stitch and other textile processes, such as appliqué, chain-hooking and stitching, French or spool knitting, felting and crochet, to achieve rich and tactile surfaces. Creating experimental sample areas can often inform and inspire a larger scale piece of work, and this process can certainly be useful to try out preliminary ideas.

Be prepared to try less conventional materials, and combinations of techniques and processes, exploring different heights, scales and textural possibilities within your work. It is useful to observe and note how different fabrics and fibres behave, individually and when combined with others. For instance, the loops of an area of hooked felt fabric will be more solid, sturdy and vertical than those done with nylon or polyester. Certain printed fabrics, because of the twist that occurs from time to time when hooking, will occasionally expose the paler version on their reverse side, creating an overall tonal appearance. As well as patterned fabrics, batiked and silk-painted swatches, and space-dyed yarns can generate unusual marks and colourings in your work. Frayed edges of furnishing linens and novelty yarns produce interesting irregular surfaces; using pinking shears to trim the ends of a prodded area or to cut the entire pieces of fabric will produce a serrated textural surface. You could try waxed paper, cellophane, balloons, foam rubber, raffia and straw, fur, outdated bank notes, and gauzy plastic satsuma packaging. Once again, part of the fun with this medium will be the rummaging and collecting.

Embellishment

Scribbled net

White or cream polyester, nylon net and certain synthetic lace fabrics work best with this process. Use fabric crayons and markers applied directly on to the fabric. Make random marks with your colours, leaving enough of the fabric blank to contrast. Fix the 'scribbled' design by applying a hot iron to the reverse of the fabric, according to the

41 *Hooked silk fabrics and raised wrapped wire loops of textured and space-dyed yarns.*

42 *A wide variety of fabrics and fibres, including net, foil-printed Lycra, pierced rubber and ric-rac braid, combined with beading and wire wrapping.*

43 *Fleece sculpting and wire wrapping encased by prodded hand-painted silk.*

44 *Stitched decorative braids echoing the printed silver Lycra.*

41

42

43

44

45

manufacturer's instructions. Cut pieces for prodding from your fabric with scissors. Because of the nature of the fabric and the unpredictability of the marks, you will find that you can achieve a lovely ethereal quality with scribbled net.

Heat-bonding

All sorts of leftover papers, threads, tiny fabric offcuts, sequins and small beads can be used here. To enable these to bond, an assortment of plastic-based materials such as bubble wrap, laminating pouches, plastic bath scrubs and other waste material can be used. On top of a thick towel and a sheet of non-stick baking parchment, create a layered 'sandwich' of these materials, strategically arranging colours and shapes. Make the work slightly bigger than the shape that you ultimately want. Place over this another sheet of non-stick baking parchment, and iron on top with a hot iron. Once it has sufficiently melted and slightly cooled, peel the baking parchment away from the plastic and trim the shape to size. These can then be used between areas of hooking, attaching with an all-purpose adhesive, or by making holes with a thick needle and applying them like buttons.

Shisha mirrors

Although bought shisha mirrors are available in different sizes, you can also achieve the look by saving tiny mirror offcuts or applying tin foil to card circles and completing the effect of both these options with an outer plastic or metal ring, bound with beautiful threads or narrow strips of fabric such as silk. The ring should be wrapped similarly to the wire-wrapping technique. The excess thread should be used to neatly stitch or couch the embellishment in place, on top of or within the hooked area.

45 *Scribbled net.*

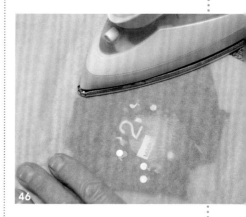

46 *Heat-bonding.*

▶ NOTE
Heat-bonding should always be done in a well-ventilated area, and you should wear a protective mask against any toxic fumes.

47 *Securing the outlined shisha mirror.*

Pompoms and bobbles

These can be bought in various sizes and colours. However, for edging or embellishing a rug or wall hanging, you can make your own in a variety of ways. They can be wet-felted, using hot soapy water and moulded in your hands. For needle-felted pompoms, I use carpet wool thrums for the core: create a spherical shape by winding the wool around your finger until you have the desired size. Place fleece around this sphere and use a felting needle (see page 42) to lock the fibres and create a smooth, solid ball. This can be left plain or decorated with stitch, beads or sequins, or with needle-felted detail.

48

48 *Needle-felting a spherical shape.*

Alternatively, you can use strips of pure woollen woven or knitted fabric, such as a mohair scarf or blanket. The strip width should be in accordance with the chosen size of your pompom. Once you have made the required number of spheres, place them, one at a time, inside an old pair of tights, separating them with tightly knotted yarn. Set them on the hottest wash cycle of your machine, together with a coarse item, such as a towel, for friction. Pompoms can also be made in the traditional way, so favoured in primary-school projects.

49

Junk jewellery, shells, glass, pebble or slate slices, and dyed, sanded coconut shell are among the many items which might be used to embellish and enhance a piece of non-functional work. They can be glued or stitched into the textile in a variety of ways.

49 *Different sizes of felted balls using a variety of methods.*

Dyeing

Although for me part of the pleasure in making rag rugs is in the sourcing and collecting of a diversity of fabrics, experimenting with dyeing and overdyeing fabrics can be fun, and can produce a range of interesting and closely-related tones and hues which might otherwise be hard to find.

Natural and synthetic dyes are derived from animals, plants and minerals, for example cochineal, kermes, indigo, onion skins, iron buff and ochre. Possibilities within the plant category are enormous and often easily accessible, such as nettles, oak bark, horse chestnuts and blackberries. Chemical dyes are relatively inexpensive and labour saving. Acid dyes are water soluble and work well with wool, silk and hairy fibres.

All colours can be mixed from the basic primary colours – red, yellow and blue – with or without the addition of black. Adding more of a dye's complementary colour to a dye bath will darken or tone down the eventual colour. Similarly, many fabrics can be overdyed in a weak or light dye bath to mute or transform their existing colours. To achieve an uneven, mottled effect, the space for the amount of fabric within the dye bath should be cramped.

The existing colour of a fabric can be removed by immersing it in a simmering solution of ammonia for a few minutes. Fabric can be simmered for approximately half an hour, in a solution of either salt or vinegar, in order to set a new colour, making it dye-fast. Salt opens the pores of the fabric, increasing its ability to absorb the dye, and also dulls colour, whereas vinegar will brighten and enhance it. It should finally be rinsed well. This process has better results with predominantly natural fibres. There are also commercial dye removers, if the colour is hard to extract.

Direct dyes, for all natural fabrics including wool, cotton, silk, straw and linen, can be ideal for rag rugs and wall hangings. Disperse dyes, including the stove-top variety, are suited to synthetic fabrics and fibres. Fibre-reactive Procion dyes which, like acid dyes, are normally supplied in the form of granules or powder, include both hot- and cold-water methods. The processes, done either by hand or in a washing machine, are suitable for natural fibres, and have the highest rate of adherence. Cold-water dyes have the advantage of being usable outdoors. The intensity of the range of colours can easily be adjusted by the strength of the dyebath. Tie-dye and batik effects can be achieved with cold-water dyeing, and can sometimes be done in a microwave, where a mottled or uneven appearance can be obtained, if desired. Some multi-purpose dyes may be suitable for materials including leather, Lycra, raffia and plastics.

If the dyeing process as a preliminary task appeals, it can be both fascinating and helpful to keep a record of your dyeing experiments. Note the type of dye, fabric or fibre type, dyeing time, any pre-treatments, and number of immersions, accompanied by a small swatch of the achieved colour. Also, if you know that certain household or clothing items are not dye-fast and will bleed their colours when washed, you might wish to experimentally place some fabrics together with these in a machine wash, finally fixing them with your chosen method. This can often result in a range of paler, subtle tones, both on plain and patterned fabrics. Just as kippers were once used to extract fabric dyes for rag rugs, it is perfectly possible, with the addition of salt, to make a dyebath from the contents of your fruit bowl, vegetable rack or kitchen cupboards, such as saffron, turmeric, red cabbage, beetroot, spinach, kale, certain fruit skins, coffee and tea.

Other useful equipment includes an enamel pot, to be used solely for dyeing, measuring spoons and cups, rods and dowels, a heatproof measuring jug, wide-necked plastic-lidded storage jars, labels, rubber gloves and a notebook. It is advisable to wear old clothes and an apron, and depending on the dye, a facemask. Work in a well-ventilated area. For disposal, dye solutions should be diluted and poured down an outside drain.

Finishing

How you finish your project will depend largely on its size and function.

Finishing a rug

It has always been debatable whether a rug should be backed. Backing a rug with hessian can be problematic, since dirt and grit can settle between the two layers, adversely affecting the right side. However, coating the back of the rug first with latex adhesive will help to prevent this, and will also prevent any loops or tufts from disappearing. As appropriate, hessian, felt or heavy cotton can be used for backing. For smaller items, such as pictures or jewellery, a softer material can be used.

When backing a rug, carpet-binding tape can be used but as it shrinks considerably, should always be washed first. It can be dyed to match the colour of your work. Take your rug off the frame, if used, trimming around the edges so that there is a backing cloth excess of 5–7.5 cm (2–3 in). Turn this under all the way round, bonding it to the reverse with latex. Having cut and hemmed the edges of a slightly smaller piece of backing cloth, position this on top of the reverse, attaching the two surfaces with latex. If necessary, complete the process by gluing carpet binding all the way round the reverse of the rug, mitring the corners.

Finishing a wall hanging

If you are attaching a wall hanging to mounting board and framing, no backing is necessary. To finish a smaller pictorial piece, turn in the backing cloth approximately 2.5 cm (1 in) beyond the outer edge of the design, all the way round the work. With small stitches, sew carefully from the right side, between any loops or tufts. Spread latex adhesive thinly across the reverse and allow to dry.

Back a wall hanging with a heavy, durable fabric, allowing enough for a hem. Avoid making this too taut as this will prevent the piece from hanging properly. Placing the backing on the reverse, pin along each turned-under edge, mitring the corners. Stitch the edges neatly with strong thread.

Another hanging method is to stitch strong tape loops or create a further long fabric sleeve along the top of the reverse, through which a batten or pole can be slotted. Heavy-duty Velcro, stitched to both ends of the textile's reverse and attached to battens which are fixed to the wall is another successful option.

50 *Batten slotted through an extra sleeve in the lining of the wall hanging.*

Cleaning and care

Surface dust and grime can be carefully removed with a low-suction vacuum cleaner attachment. If the work is very delicate and incorporates an assortment of fabrics and fibres. a sheet or nylon monofilament screen can be placed over an area as you clean. However, if the fabrics are more durable, and the reverse has been latexed, protecting the weaker hessian threads, the work can be gently shaken outside. Any spills or staining should be tackled immediately with a towel or absorbent kitchen paper, sponging with lukewarm water, taking care not to over-moisten the fibres. A weak solution of white vinegar or household ammonia should remove any difficult stains. When not in use, your rugs should be rolled with the top surface facing outwards, and stored in a dry environment, within layers of bubblewrap, and an outer cotton bag.

Recycle, upcycle…

5

I would be the first to admit that I can get some very strange looks as I scrutinise skips, gape longingly at litter, and wander apparently aimlessly through supermarket aisles, scanning the shelves not so much for delectable edibles, as for the most interesting beer bottle tops and colourful printed foil biscuit wrappers!

The notion of turning trash into treasure is a magical one which exists at the very heart of creativity. With open eyes and mind, new, stylish and often witty uses can be found and fashioned from reclaimed, everyday and often unremarkable objects. The idea of these having had a previous life, with a story to tell, often provides the necessary spark and stimulus for a new creation.

Rejected and unwanted items, given a different context, can very often have a fresh aesthetic appeal, revealing attractive qualities with essentially human connections. The surface of a recycled pre-loved object may be worn and withered, rusted or corroded, its painted or printed image perhaps blurred or faded, inviting subtle transformation or an entirely new identity by the addition of different materials and processes.

Recycling and upcycling are activities associated with thrift. There is a certain freedom in making, afforded by the fact that these articles often come at little or no financial cost, allowing playful experimentation and mistakes to be made. It is often, in my experience, those mistakes which end up being the most fruitful!

In tune with the times, this area of recycling is also eco-friendly and beneficial for the environment, creatively addressing issues connected with sustainable living and waste management, even if in a relatively small way.

Undoubtedly, a vital aspect of rag-rug making will involve sourcing and using a rich diversity of recycled fabrics. Browsing in charity and thrift shops will occasionally introduce you to items of clothing which, at first sight, in their original state, may seem ugly and outdated. However, the inclusion of such fabrics often provides unexpected richness. A worn and unattractive jacket may have wonderful vintage Bakelite buttons; a belt buckle may be just the shape you were looking for. Interesting embroidered or printed patches or labels might provide inspiration; knitwear can be felted in a hot machine wash, or simply unravelled to re-use the yarn. But this is far from the end of the story! I hope that many of the examples and projects shown in this book will fire your imagination and help you to consider the vast range of commonplace objects that, instead of being discarded, could be incorporated within your work in the most personal and exciting ways.

Even rag-rug tools and backing cloths, as history has already indicated, can be fashioned from existing objects. I have found that a lacquered chopstick can be a fine tool for prodding, and a vegetable sack, as well as providing suitable backing cloth, might inspire a piece of work because of its attractive printed design. Plastic building and garden meshes can also have their uses, particularly for an exterior project, which might involve using recycled packaging for the 'weft' materials.

51 Ben Hall, *Café do Brasil. Hooked without a frame. Coloured denim, cotton, leather, tea-dyed wool blanket strips.*

52 **Kaisa Takala, Minna Piironen, Hanna-Liisa Pykala,** *Postcard from Helsinki, 2010. Knotted plastic packaging waste around construction mesh.*

When thinking about decorative patterns and borders, the flotsam and jetsam seen during a walk on the beach, as well as interesting pieces of beached glass, shells, pebbles, feathers, driftwood and stones, can inform and contribute to a piece of work. Ring-pulls from cans, sliced corks, and inverted or hammered bottle tops can all be useful additions. Sanded pieces of dried coconut shell, painted with acrylics or dyed with wood stains, drilled and stitched, or attached to your backing cloth with adhesive, create a rich surface when encased within hooked fabrics and beadwork. Junk jewellery, buttons and beads, and also glass nuggets used for floristry provide decorative interest and texture; curtain rings can be wrapped with thread or fabric, covering pieces of mirror or foil-covered card, to mimic shisha mirrors.

Parts of toys, such as a small car wheel or a doll's head or even a painted zoo or farmyard animal, might all prove to be exciting finds. Household articles that have seen better days, such as old faded tea towels, a crocheted doily, metal pan scourers and plastic bath scrubs, might all find their way into your work. Trays, picture frames and painting canvases might be suitable for mounting or framing a pictorial piece, while metal and plastic bottle and carton tops or other elements of packaging could be salvaged, for containing tiny badges and buttons, or as decorative elements within a larger piece of work.

As you saw in the Embellishment section on pages 44–47, many materials, objects and artefacts can be reworked and transformed. Many polymer-based materials, once heat is applied, will shrink, blister and laminate, and experimentation can lead to the creation of interesting buttons, beads and other forms.

Fruit punnets and containers, and small glass herb pots can be useful for storing buttons, beads, junk jewellery and other embellishment items.

The creative potential involving reclaimed, recycled and upcycled materials is infinite. As well as helping to make this an accessible and inexpensive craft, it is challenging to fashion something which is certainly unique, whilst giving value and new meaning to 'clutter'.

53 **Lynne Stein,** *rug sample. Hooked biscuit wrappers, sanded and dyed coconut shell beading and stitched ric-rac braid.*

53

The creative eye: sources of inspiration

6

Any number of articles and objects can provide starting points for your work. These might include printed material such as greetings cards and wrapping papers, patterns on clothing and furnishing fabrics, jewellery design, and ceramic decoration, or a section of a painting, whether detailed and figurative or bold and abstract.

Selecting the appropriate rag-rug technique for a specific project is vital to the ultimate appearance of your work, and since hooking and prodding create quite different surfaces and textures, such decisions might be important at the early stages of your design process. For example, if a blurred and rather Impressionistic appearance is desired, the prodded technique would be more suitable. If great definition and detail are required, hooking is the more usual choice. However, as shown throughout this book, a range of techniques can be introduced and combined with each other to suit a project, the choices being influenced both functionally and aesthetically.

Narratives in the form of song lyrics, legends, nursery rhymes, poems or stories might inspire you, just as a piece of family memorabilia might spark off the core of an idea.

Visiting galleries and museums will offer endless opportunities for browsing through collections and discovering works of aesthetic appeal and personal relevance. Different seasons will allow you to focus on the shifting shapes and tones of landscape and nature. Rows of vegetables growing in an urban allotment might provide the focus for stylised rhythmic and repetitive patterns, and summer gardens in full bloom can serve as a reminder and living proof of the magic of colour.

54

Many of the people who have attended my workshops over the years have been keen to depict their domestic pets, a marmalade cat, or on one memorable occasion, a pot-bellied pig! A trip to the zoo or an aquarium can be a wonderful way of engaging children in drawing activities, which can in turn inspire your own work. As I frequently emphasise, children's art can be perfectly suited to this medium, and drawings from my own children provided me with wonderful mermaids and spotted mythical beasts, far more expressive and exotic than I could possibly have imagined on my own!

Rusted, corroded and decaying objects and surfaces display interesting tones and textures for translation into abstract patterns and designs for rugs. Aerial photography exposing the shapes and textures of farmed and furrowed fields can also be the stimulus for abstract works.

Since the medium is not restricted to creating purely two-dimensional surfaces, decorative three-dimensional objects can be made, with thematic possibilities ranging from birds and fertility dolls to a fancy gateau!

54 Lynne Stein, *La Mer* (detail), 1990. *128 x 126 cm (50 ½ x 49 ½ in). Gun-tufted. (An electrical tufting gun speedily inserts loops of adjustable height into a cloth. Resembling the appearance of hooking, it allows for very fine and compact work.) Largely recycled fabrics and fibres on polyester backing cloth. Always working from the reverse of the backing cloth, the tufting gun enables a mosaic-like surface to be created, allowing the inclusion of relief convex surfaces.*

55 Lynne Stein, *Pathway Well Worn* (detail), 2008. *132 x 84 cm (52 x 33 in). Hand-hooked, needle-felting, stitch. Largely recycled mixed fabrics and fibres, plastics, rubber, paper.*

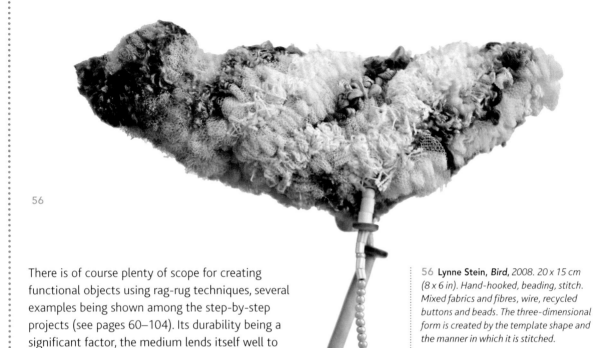

56

There is of course plenty of scope for creating functional objects using rag-rug techniques, several examples being shown among the step-by-step projects (see pages 60–104). Its durability being a significant factor, the medium lends itself well to all manner of projects, from bolster cushions to doorstops and draught excluders. In this instance, you may find that the idea of making a certain article well is your prime motivation.

Inspiration may be generated by a lucky find of fabrics or embellishment artefacts, which you feel compelled to incorporate. Unusual vintage buttons or a flamboyant floral fabric can frequently prompt my designs for a new creation! Being prepared to 'play' with a selection of fabrics and fibres of a chosen palette, and being sensitive to their qualities, will dictate and lead to a more developed design, and is very akin to the process of painting, in a fluid and highly intuitive way.

If you are happy and relatively confident with drawing and painting materials, keeping a sketchbook is an ideal way of recording, developing and experimenting with ideas for your work. Of course, tracing and copying are also possible, and it is simple enough to reduce or enlarge a design. I often find that making collages of my designs can be a more freeing preliminary process, bearing a certain compatibility to the medium of rag-rug making. Just as I store fabrics, I also salvage the colourful pages of glossy magazines and my own photographic images for this process. Keeping scrapbooks and moodboards, where colour schemes, embellishment details, fabric swatches, photographs, and mere doodles can all be registered, is of great value.

56 **Lynne Stein**, *Bird*, *2008. 20 x 15 cm (8 x 6 in). Hand-hooked, beading, stitch. Mixed fabrics and fibres, wire, recycled buttons and beads. The three-dimensional form is created by the template shape and the manner in which it is stitched.*

57

58

57 *Reassembled and collaged cut and torn prints from the author's photograph collection.*

58 *Collage using stitched paper, magazine and wrapping paper and photographic print.*

The Internet provides an inexhaustible and invaluable source of information, both textual and visual, and as well as providing a wealth of interesting images, is also capable of helping you to solve logistical problems and locate suppliers for any of your textile-related needs. Digital photography, scanning and manipulation of photographs, and various drawing and painting software programmes, along with a hand-held tablet computer, are extremely useful design aids. Many mobile phones have an integrated camera, so recording and collating visual references is now a simple and direct procedure, getting you into the habit of seeking out aesthetically interesting objects and situations.

Projects

7

1. Allotment veggie markers

This simple way to use and recycle shopping bags could be adapted to various vegetables and salad crops, and will be an instant reminder of sowing positions, as well as a bold and quirky way of jazzing up the veggie plot.

You will need:

- plastic carrier bags: 4 orange, 3 dark green, 3 lime green – all cut into 1.5 cm (½ in) strips
- 45 cm (½ yd) black woven polypropylene horticultural plastic
- 2 plastic-coated garden stakes

- 45 cm (½ yd) wire
- 2 small plastic storage crates with 25 x 14 cm (10 x 5 in) bases
- indelible white marker pen
- indelible black marker pen
- packaging tape

- scissors
- quilting hoop
- rug hook
- latex adhesive, spreader
- needle
- plastic-coated wire

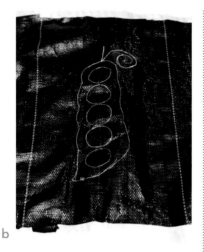

b

c.1

c.2

e

a. Cut the horticultural plastic in two, lengthways. Tape around all four sides of each piece, to prevent it from fraying.

b. Draw the carrot and peapod shapes on each piece with your white marker.

c. Insert the carrot design sheet securely into your quilting hoop. Hook the entire shape finely and tightly so that it is very compact, making the loops of the green leaf shapes slightly longer. Shear the loops of the leaves so that there is textural contrast between the two areas. Take the design out of the hoop and set aside.

d. Insert the pea-pod design sheet into your hoop. Again, hook the whole design tightly, working on the circular lime green pea shapes first.

e. Remove the design from the hoop, trimming the excess plastic to 2.5 cm (1 in) beyond the outer edge of the hooked shape and snipping it close to the hooking line at intervals. Working from the front of the design, fold behind the excess plastic and stitch it carefully in place, ensuring that the vegetable shape is precise.

f. To make one of the tendrils, fold 15 cm (6 in) of wire double and wrap it tightly with a long strip of dark green plastic (see Techniques, page 41), securing the end by threading it back through the inside of the wrapped tube.

g. To make the thinner spiral stem, repeat this process, using only a single 30 cm (12 in) length of wire. Once the wire is bound with the plastic and secured, bend it into a spiral.

h. Attach both wrapped wire pieces to the back of the peapod, by stitching them securely into position, again working from the front so that none of your hooking is dislodged.

i. Repeat step e. for the carrot. Spread latex on the reverse side of both shapes and allow to dry.

j. Cut the bases from the plastic crates, and draw with the black marker around your carrot and peapod templates on each. Cut these out with heavy-duty scissors. At the upper centre of both shapes, pierce four holes, to form a rectangle, accommodating the width of the stakes.

k. Spread latex thinly across the top of both bases, and press each hooked shape on top, carefully lining them up. Allow to dry.

l. Thread the plastic-coated wire into a sharp needle, stitching carefully through the pierced holes and hooked surfaces, and securing the veggie markers to the stakes by knotting them tightly at the back several times.

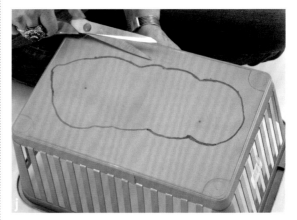

2. Christmas stocking

Roomy enough for those foil-wrapped tangerines as well as the more precious pressies, this will become an heirloom piece for passing down through the generations.

You will need:

- tracing paper
- pencil
- indelible marker
- transfer pencil
- pins
- hessian (approx. 72 cm (28 in) square)
- iron, pressing cloth
- frame
- drawing pins or staple gun and staples
- rug hook
- scissors
- bodkin, needles, thread
- flexible wire or scoobies
- latex adhesive, spreader
- large piece of felt, 56 cm (22 in) square
- assorted fabrics, cut into long strips, 1.5 cm (½ in) wide
- pink and brown yarns
- green braided piping cord, 137 cm (54 in)
- buttons, beads, toy eyes, silver bell, buckle
- small amount of pink fleece
- felting needle, size 36/38
- felting sponge

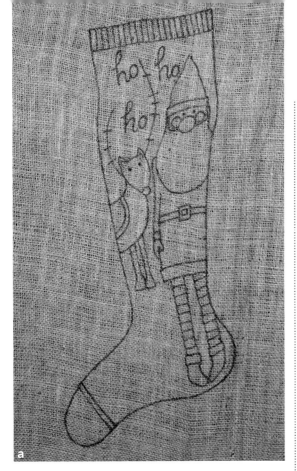

a. Draw the 48 x 28 cm (19 x 11 in) stocking shape on tracing paper. Reversing the paper, draw over the design with a transfer pencil. Pin the paper, transfer side face down, onto your hessian. Keeping both hessian and paper flat, cover them with a cloth and go over the design with a hot iron, transferring the image onto the hessian. Remove the paper and clarify the image with a marker. Attach the hessian tightly to a frame, ensuring that the design is positioned centrally and not distorted.

b. Using a sturdy fabric such as felted knitwear for the background, start hooking, pulling the loops to a height of 0.5 cm (¼ in).

c. The lettering should be hooked using black stretchy material, such as tights.

d. Santa's beard can be hooked in knitwear, varying the loop height to maximise texture, and his cheeks hooked in wool, shearing the loops.

e. Using a felting needle and pink fleece (see Techniques, page 42), shape Santa's nose.

f. Work the reindeer's antlers by wrapping wire with woollen yarn (see Techniques, page 41), securing them by couching with the same wool.

g. Stitch the bell, nose, lace trim, buckle, eye beads and buttons in place.

h. Unpin the hessian and cut out the stocking, leaving a 2.5 cm (1 in) border. Snip the border close to the hooking line at intervals, folding the overlap back on the reverse and stitching it in place from the front. Spread latex thinly over the reverse of the stocking. Leave to dry overnight.

i. Using the stocking as your template, cut 2 additional shapes out of felt. Use one piece for lining the hooked stocking, and the second for lining the stocking's back.

j. Cut out a slightly larger duplicate shape for the stocking's back from a sturdy and suitably coloured fabric, leaving an additional seam allowance. Stitch a hem at the top.

k. Stitch the second felt lining shape to the reverse of the stocking's back. Turning in the seam allowance, stitch the stocking's back to the hooked front, adjusting the shape to fit.

l. Apply latex to each end and allow it to dry, then stitch the piping cord around the stocking's edge, concealing the ends inside the stocking and leaving enough at the right side for a hanging loop.

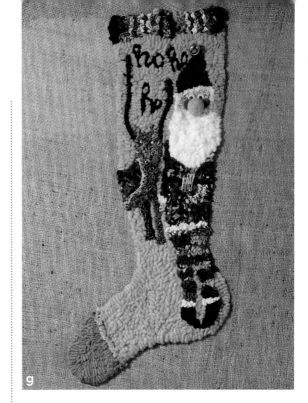

3. Flower power garland

This idea can also be adapted for a Christmas wreath, using different fabrics and colours, and perhaps substituting cinnamon sticks and candy canes for the butterfly, for a more seasonal feel. The individual flowers could make a lovely brooch or corsage. Several floral patterned fabrics – all charity shop finds – have been used for maximum effect.

You will need:

- metal coat hanger
- frame
- hessian to fit
- prodder
- rug hook
- scissors
- needles, threads
- lime green patterned cotton fabrics, cut into 10 x 2.5 cm (4 x 1 in) pieces

- colourful and floral fabrics, cut into 7.5 x 2.5 cm (3 x 1 in) pieces
- 92 cm (36 in) checked nylon ribbon, cut into 6.5 cm (2½ in) pieces
- 1 square of yellow felt, cut into 6.5 x 2 cm (2½ x ¾ in) pieces
- white net, 45 cm (½ yd)
- fabric markers
- nylon wire

- 14 small dark beads, 2 small silver beads
- brown and beige woollen yarns
- 3 coloured buttons
- felting needle, size 36/38
- felting sponge
- brown and red unspun fleece, small amounts
- latex adhesive, spreader

a. Bend the coat hanger into a circle, retaining the hook for hanging. Work the green fabric strips in a closely packed row around your circle, tying each tightly with a simple knot to secure, and leaving the hook uncovered. Trim any irregularities to maintain a pleasing shape.

b. On your stretched hessian draw 6 well-spaced circles, ranging from 2.5 to 5 cm (1 to 2 in) in diameter. Additionally, draw the shape of a butterfly body.

a

c

d

c. Selecting combinations of fabrics to give each flower a different colour, work each of the circles with your prodder, starting from the outside of each, and packing your prodding quite tightly, working towards the centres.

d. Using at least 4 strands of wool simultaneously, hook the butterfly's body, alternating the beige and brown stripes and leaving your loops considerably longer and packed tightly together. This should be sheared and sculpted with sharp scissors (see Techniques, page 41).

e. Scribble across your net fabric with fabric markers, leaving enough of its natural colour exposed (see Embellishment, page 44). Cut the net into 10 x 2.5 cm (4 x1 in) pieces, and hook enough of these along each side of the butterfly's body to resemble its wings. Trim them to further define their shape.

f. Cut out each circle leaving an overlap of 1.5 cm (½ in), which should be stitched in place on the reverse and spread with a thin layer of latex. Treat the butterfly shape in the same way. Leave to dry.

e

g. Turn the circles over and trim to define satisfactory floral shapes. Sew buttons in the centres of three flowers.

h. With your felting needle, sponge and red fleece, create a small spherical shape to be stitched in the centre of one of the other flowers (see Techniques, page 42).

i. Also with your needle-felting tools, create a small brown head for the butterfly. Stitch this to the top of the body, applying silver beads for its eyes, and small dark beads threaded on nylon wire for its antennae.

j. Stitch strong thread through the reverse of each individual shape, and tie tightly into their required positions around the garland. Trim any excess threads on the reverse.

4. Fried egg pot holder

This bold graphic design is a witty way of ensuring that you don't burn your fingers when cooking the breakfast!

You will need:

- quilting hoop
- hessian
- rug hook
- bowls or plates for circular templates, 25 and 9 cm (10 and 3½ in) radius
- scissors
- indelible marker
- wide-eyed needle, needles and threads, pins
- white and yellow t-shirt fabric, cut into 1.5 cm (½ in) strips

- yellow towelling fabric, 25 cm (10 in) radius circle plus 0.5 cm (¼ in) overlap
- white lining fabric, 2 x 25 cm (10 in) radius circles plus 0.5 cm (¼ in) overlap
- colour co-ordinated ribbon, 15 cm (6 in) length
- Domette interlining fabric or heat-resistant batting, 2 circles to fit

a. Draw your fried egg shape on the hessian, making the outer circle slightly irregular.

b. Insert the hessian into your hoop, ensuring that it is sufficiently taut.

c. Begin by hooking the entire egg-yolk shape at the centre, keeping your loops as compact and even as possible.

d. Hook closely around this with white t-shirt fabric, maintaining the same appearance.

e. When the whole shape is filled in, remove it from the hoop and trim around the design, leaving an excess of 2.5 cm (1 in).

f. Turn the excess to the reverse side of the design and tack it in place from the front. Lightly latex over the raw edge of the hessian and leave to dry.

g. With a long strip of the white fabric, oversew to bind the outer shape of the fried egg.

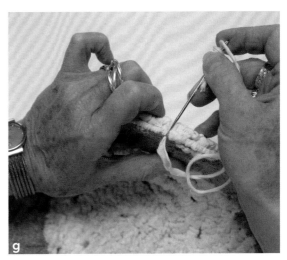

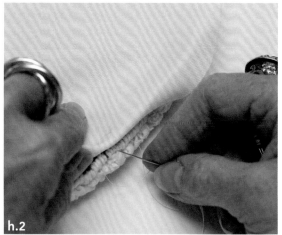

h. Sandwich a circle of Domette interlining fabric between the reverse of the fried egg shape and a circle of the lining fabric, and hem the lining in place.

i. Likewise, sandwich Domette between the towelling and lining circles and hem into place.

j. Place the fried egg shape over the towelling circle, with the lining fabrics facing each other on the inside. Neatly oversew the two shapes together, leaving an opening you can comfortably get your hand into. Insert the folded ribbon loop opposite the opening and stitch into place.

5. Hair accessories

The template for each hair decoration is a very simple shape, and each can be hooked or prodded on a quilting hoop. I have included delicate sequined fabrics, metallic lurex and ribbons to achieve the glitzy effect in each, but you may wish to use entirely different fabrics for these pieces. The ideas could be scaled down in size for little girls, made into brooches, or stitched as decorations for pull-on hats, bags or pockets.

You will need:

- Alice band, hair comb, hair clip
- card
- 8 cm (3 in) diameter circular object
- pencil, ruler, indelible marker
- quilting hoop
- hessian, 45 cm (½ yd)
- extra-fine rug hook
- woollen knitwear and assorted fabrics
- scissors
- latex adhesive, spreader
- felt or wool, small piece
- needles, pins, strong thread
- sequins
- felting needle, size 36/38
- felting sponge

Hair clip

a. Cut an oval card template, slightly bigger than the outer shape of your hair clip. With your marker, draw around this on the hessian, and insert it in your quilting hoop, ensuring that it is taut, for ease of hooking.

b. Hook the shape with narrow strips of sequinned fabric.

c. Cut out the finished shape, leaving a 1.5 cm (½ in) border. Tuck in the overlap on the reverse of the work and stitch this in place, working from the front.

d. Spread latex on the reverse side, allowing it to dry overnight.

e. Line the reverse with felt or woollen cloth, and stitch the hair clip securely in place.

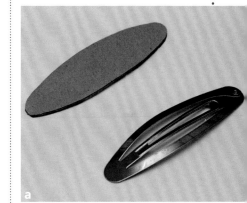

Hair comb

a. Cut a rectangular card template measuring 8 x 5 cm (3 x 2 in), or slightly broader than your comb. Cut a heart template to fit within the shape.

b. Draw around these on the hessian, placing the heart centrally within the rectangle. Insert the hessian in your quilting hoop.

c. Hook the rectangular shape with narrow strips of stretchy lurex, working around the heart shape.

d. Hook the heart shape with narrow gold ribbon, carefully shearing the loops once you have completed the shape.

e. Repeat the same finishing process as previously, finally stitching the rectangular shape onto the comb.

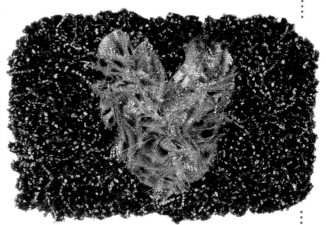

Alice band

a. Using an 8 cm (3 in) diameter object as your template, draw the circular shape onto your hessian. Insert the hessian into your quilting hoop.

b. Hook the shape in concentric circles using a combination of 1.5 cm (½ in) strips of recycled woollen knitwear and decorative ribbons. Leave your loops slightly longer towards the outer edge. Trim them all, sculpting the whole shape.

c. Cut a long 1.5 cm (½ in) strip of knitwear and wind it around your finger into a tight sphere. Use a felting needle to perfect its shape.

d. Sew this into the centre of your circular shape, decorating it with a few stitched sequins.

e. Take a long 2.5 cm (1 in) strip of knitwear fabric and bind the Alice band tightly in a diagonal direction, stitching it at each end.

f. Repeat the same finishing processes as for the other hair accessories, and stitch your circle securely into an off-centre position on your Alice band.

d

e

Photograph by Joel Stein.

75

6. 'Home is where the hearts are!'

This draught excluder is made using a locker hook, which gives it a particularly sturdy and durable quality. Although a more time-consuming project, it is easily portable, and can be made with minimal expense while watching TV!

You will need:

- 45 cm (½ yd) of 1 m (40 in) rug canvas (3 holes to 1 in)
- locker hook
- scissors
- assorted needles, pins
- assorted durable fabrics, including felt, t-shirts, velour
- rug yarn, strong twine, cotton

- coloured pencils, paper, tracing paper, dressmaker's carbon paper, thin card
- indelible marker
- lining material, 96 x 25 cm (38 x 10 in)

- backing fabric 107 x 38 cm (42 x 15 in)
- 91 cm (36 in) draught excluder inner pad
- 270 cm (3 yds) mini-pompom braid
- 3 press studs

a. Within an outer rectangle 22 x 94 cm (8½ x 37 in), trace your design from its original drawing, using card templates for the hearts and letters if necessary. Use a variety of fonts if preferred. Transfer the traced design directly onto the rug canvas using dressmaker's carbon paper. Clarify the design with a marker pen.

a.1

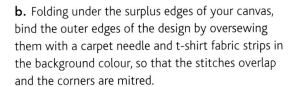

b. Folding under the surplus edges of your canvas, bind the outer edges of the design by oversewing them with a carpet needle and t-shirt fabric strips in the background colour, so that the stitches overlap and the corners are mitred.

c. Cut long fabric strips in 2 cm (¾ in) widths, depending on their quality and thickness, aiming to cover the rug canvas mesh and holes.

d. Thread a good length of rug yarn through the eye of your locker needle hook. Holding your fabric strip under the canvas, use the forefinger of your other hand to poke the hooked part of the locker needle through a hole, catching a loop of the fabric from underneath and pulling it up through the canvas (see Techniques, page 40). Work from right to left, trying to ensure that your loops are even.

e. Hook approximately ten loops at a time onto your needle, pulling it through the loops so that the yarn anchors them in place. Repeat this process until each shape is filled in with the appropriate colour, including the paler background area.

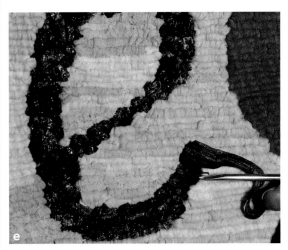

f. Turn your finished design over and lay your lining fabric on top of the reverse, turning under the raw edges. Slip stitch the lining in place around all four sides of the design.

g. Stitch the pompom braid around the entire outer edge of the design's front surface.

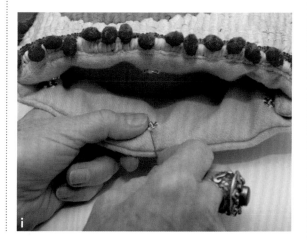

h. Turning under the raw edges of your backing fabric, create a 2.5 cm (1 in) double-turn hem along one of the short ends. Neatly slip stitch the other three sides to the bound edges of the rug canvas, inserting the cushion pad before you finish stitching the third side.

i. Stitch the press studs in place in evenly-spaced corresponding positions along both inner sides of the cover.

7. Hooked and braided rug

Combining two traditional rug-making techniques as well as decorative embellishment, this rug is both pretty and practical.

You will need:

Hooked area:

- rug frame, trestles
- 92 cm (1 yd) hessian
- 92 cm (1 yd) hessian or lining fabric
- rug hook
- scissors
- assorted non-fraying fabrics, ribbons and yarns
- needles, strong thread, black cotton thread, pins

- dyed fleece, assorted colours, small amounts
- felting needle, size 36/38
- felting sponge
- button
- indelible marker, pencil
- tracing paper, transfer pencil, ruler
- pressing cloth, iron
- latex adhesive, spreader

Braided border:

- 3 flat woollen fabrics, each 264 x 5 cm (104 x 2 in) wide
- tape measure, ruler
- scissors or rotary cutter and mat
- carpet needle
- large kilt safety pin

a. Draw the design for the hooked part of the rug onto tracing paper, within its outer measurement of 77 x 52 cm (30 x 20 ½ in). Reverse the paper and draw over the design with a transfer pencil. Pin the paper transfer side down onto the hessian, keeping both surfaces flat. Cover with a cloth and go over the design with a hot iron, transferring the image onto the hessian. Remove the paper and clarify the image with your marker.

b. Attach the hessian to your frame with strong thread and mount the frame on a pair of trestles (see Preparation, page 35).

c. Using various green fabrics for the foliage, bright colours for the flowers and sun, and glittery fabric for the flower stamens, use a contrasting blend of closely toned fabrics for the background.

d. Shear the loops on some of the stems, and hook the small flowers with colourful ribbon for textural contrast.

e. Once you have hooked the sun, secure three strands of woollen yarn to the outer edge of the circle, braiding and then couching them to form an outline. Secure any excess threads through the rug's reverse.

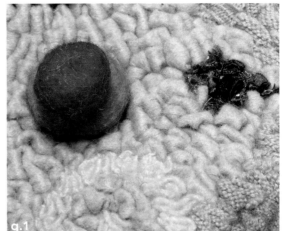

f. The animal should be hooked using closely toned fabrics, highlighting with printed fabric, and colour co-ordinated yarns for the spots. Stitch a button with black thread for the eye.

g. For additional flowers, needle-felt small spherical shapes in toning colours (see Techniques, page 42) and stitch a smaller shape on top of the larger one, stitching them through the rug.

h. Once the hooking is completed, cut your braiding fabrics into strips 5 cm (2 in) wide, giving them as much length as possible. If the lengths are shorter than 180 cm (2 yds), sew them end to end, creating neat 0.5 cm (¼ in) seams. However, to avoid bulky and uneven braids, try to stagger the position of your seams. You will need total lengths of 8.1 m (4½ yds). Your fabric strips should be rolled up and pinned to avoid becoming tangled as you braid.

i. Fasten three strips together to the large safety pin, attaching this to a static object, such as a cup hook or handle, positioned slightly above eye level. Begin braiding the strips close to the pin (see Techniques, page 43), trying to maintain an even tension, and ensuring that any raw edges are turned to the back as the braiding progresses. As the length of completed braid increases, tie it together and set it to your left as you work.

j. Once you have achieved the necessary length of braid, remove the safety pin, secure the loose ends with a pin and sew each end, tapering the braid and neatly tucking in any raw edges.

k. Keeping sufficient hessian surplus beyond your hooking, stitch the braid around the perimeter of the hooked rug, sewing edge to edge, and occasionally through the braid and the hessian surplus, with tiny stitches to maintain its position.

l. Turning the rug over, fold the surplus hessian under, so that it is just within the braid's edge, mitring corners and carefully stitching at necessary intervals. Spread a thin layer of latex across the hooked area and allow to dry overnight. Turning a small amount under on all sides, stitch your lining or hessian neatly to the rug's reverse.

8. 'It's a wrap'

This decorative piece of wall art is made almost entirely from chocolate biscuit wrappers and other recycled packaging and household items. Most of the embellishments could also be junk shop finds.

You will need:

- stretched artist's canvas 40 x 30 cm (16 x 12 in)
- frame
- hessian to fit
- indelible marker
- rug hook
- scissors
- drawing pins or staple gun and staples

- latex adhesive, spreader, all-purpose adhesive
- 2 beer bottle tops
- printed foil chocolate and biscuit wrappers
- black plastic bin liners, coloured and white plastic bags
- plastic mesh fruit bags
- plastic bath scrubs and packaging offcuts

- assorted threads and small fabric remnants
- coloured sequins, large flat beads, smaller round beads
- assorted safety pins
- iron, old towels
- non-stick baking parchment

a. With an indelible marker, draw a rectangle on your hessian, measuring the same dimensions as your artist's canvas. Divide the design into three areas, drawing a row of uneven lateral stripes within the left rectangle, and either freehand or with a card template, draw the floral shapes within the right rectangle.

b. Arrange your embellishment artefacts within the middle rectangle, and draw around these shapes. One inverted bottle top should encase one of the large flat beads, whilst the other can be flattened with a hammer to expose its design. Set these aside.

c. From an assortment of plastic bath scrubs, sequins, threads, and small plastic offcuts and fabric remnants, create areas of colourful heat-bonded plastics (see Embellishments, page 46).

d. Using the same bonding process, treat areas of hooked printed foil packaging on hessian in the same way. These can be cut into specific floral shapes, such as flower centres and petals, and a circular spiral shape, to be placed within your design and glued with an all-purpose adhesive before hooking the surrounding area.

e. With a selection of printed foil packaging for the area on the left, hook each stripe or subdivision in a different colour.

f. Using strips of white plastic 0.5 cm (¼ in) wide, hook the middle panel, working around and omitting the drawn shapes.

g. Fill the floral forms within the right rectangle with a mixture of cut heat-bonded areas and hooked strips of coloured plastic carrier bags, bath scrubs and mesh fruit bags. Some areas can be sheared or cut to create more textural contrast. Hook the background, carefully defining each shape, using narrow strips of black plastic bin liner.

h. Using all-purpose adhesive, attach the embellishment artefacts within the white hooked panel, piling smaller beads on top of the larger flat ones, and positioning the circular plastic spiral around the encased bead.

i. Once these are dry, stitch safety pins in place to resemble flower petals around the bottle top.

j. Unpinning the hessian from your frame, cut around the outer edge of the design, leaving a 2.5 cm (1 in) overlap. Turning the excess hessian to the back, stitch from the front, ensuring that there is no surplus hessian showing.

k. Trim any loose ends on the reverse, then spread latex evenly across the whole surface, and also across the canvas. Positioning the hooked design carefully on the canvas so that the edges line up, stick the two surfaces together, leaving to dry overnight.

9. Lady teacosy

Afternoon teas are back in fashion, and along with the sandwiches and cupcakes, she will add warmth and humour to any table and teapot!

You will need:

- card
- pencil, chalk, indelible marker
- drawing pins or staple gun and staples
- frame
- 2 pieces hessian to fit
- rug hook
- scissors
- needles, threads, pins
- assorted smooth fabrics, cut into 1.5 cm (½ in) strips
- small amount red knitted fabric, cut into 1.5 cm (½ in) strips
- 23 cm (¼ yd) woven mohair, cut into long strips
- tights
- latex adhesive, spreader
- lining fabric, 45 cm (½ yd)
- batting/wadding, 45 cm (½ yd)

a. Attach the hessian tightly to your frame. Draw the outer teacosy shape, either freehand or with the aid of a card template, onto the centre of your hessian with an indelible marker, ensuring it measures 35.5 x 28 cm (14 x 11 in). You will need to repeat this process on a second piece of stretched hessian once the front has been hooked, to create the teacosy's back.

b. Fill in the details of both designs freehand or with templates for the different features.

c. Using different tones of yellow and ochre fabrics, hook the hair, varying the widths of the stripes.

d. Hook the hat in bright colours that differ from the rest of the project's palette, hooking the band of the hat in lateral lines.

e. With red knitted fabric for the mouth, shear and sculpt the longer hooked loops to emphasise this feature (see Techniques, page 41).

f. Work the cheeks in concentric circles of bright pink material, and the face in flesh-coloured fabric.

g. Hook one eye in green and combine a small black button and a larger green one for the other.

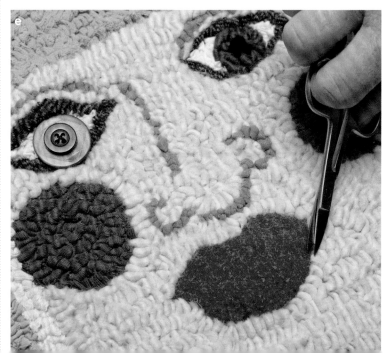

i

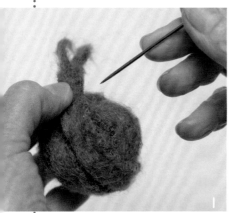

l

h. Taking care to position the hat line accurately, the teacosy back should be hooked similarly, matching the front's colours.

i. When finished, detach from the frame and cut around both shapes, leaving an overlap of 2.5 cm (1 in). Repeat steps f. and h. of the Fried egg pot holder project on page 70, leaving 1.5 cm (½ in) of the hessian exposed around the sides of each shape, apart from their straight bases.

j. Cut two template shapes of wadding, making them 1.5 cm (½ in) smaller, inserting a layer between the reverse of each teacosy shape and the lining fabric. Turn in a 1.5 cm (½ in) hem and stitch the lining in place.

k. Sew the two shapes together with strong thread, filling any gaps by overstitching with appropriate colours of fabric.

l. Cut your mohair into long enough 2.5 cm (1 in) strips to wind tightly into an 8 cm (3 in) diameter sphere, needle-felting it a little to define its shape. Knot it inside an old pair of tights and felt it in the washing machine, on a hot cycle (see Embellishments, page 47). Remove the tights, and when dry, stitch the pompom to the top of the hat with a double length of woollen yarn. N.B. If the mohair is dye-fast, you may wish to create several pompoms simultaneously, in this way, for future projects.

10. Lazy daisy chain

A pretty addition to your wardrobe, this necklace is inexpensive and simple to make, and a fine example of inventive recycling.

You will need:

- 7 flexible plastic juice carton tops, 2.5 cm (1 in) diameter
- 92 cm (1 yd) coloured twisted paper string
- 45 cm (½ yd) hessian
- orange, pink and red bouclé yarn
- knitting wool, contrasting colours

- 'jewels' or beads
- fine pencil rug hook
- scissors
- quilting hoop
- needles, thread
- latex adhesive, thin spreader
- assorted colour co-ordinated (vintage) buttons

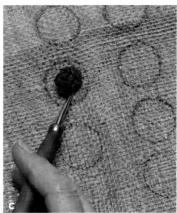

a. Use a template to draw seven 2.5 cm (1 in) diameter circles on your hessian.

b. Insert the hessian into your hoop, ensuring that it is sufficiently taut.

c. Starting from the centre of each circle, hook the shapes tightly, making two of each colour, with one extra.

d. Carefully cut each shape out, leaving a very small overlap in the hessian around them, and checking their fit within your carton top.

e. Decorate each hooked circle with contrasting wool, sewing diagonal lines which intersect at the middle.

f. Stitch a bead or diamanté 'jewel' at the centre of each circle, slightly tightening as you secure it, to maintain the detail.

g. Immediately latex the sides and reverse of each, and leave to dry.

h. Pierce two opposite sides of each carton top with a tapestry needle, and thread paper string through these holes, interspersing each cap with a few threaded coloured buttons.

i. Spread more latex on the reverse of each circle, and press each into place within the tops. The detail of each daisy can be redefined by manipulating the loops and decoration with the eye of your needle.

j. Deciding on the required length of your necklace, thread a button onto one end of the string, securing with a knot, and create an appropriately sized knotted loop at the other end to fasten.

11. Mizzy-mazzy runner

Inspired both by traditional English methods and the energetic and vibrant patterns of Berber rag rugs, with their areas of random mixed colours, this joyful runner incorporates all your family cast-offs, such as patterned socks and leggings, and dyed and felted jumpers.

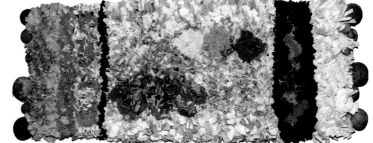

You will need:

- 2 pieces of hessian, each 92 x 45 cm (36 x 18 in)
- spring-clip tool
- assorted durable fabrics
- scissors
- fabric gauge
- large transparent plastic bags
- ruler
- tape measure
- indelible marker, chalk
- pencil, paper
- latex adhesive, spreader
- assorted needles, cotton, woollen yarn
- pins
- woven and knitted woollens, cut into strips
- old tights
- dyed merino fleece
- felting needle (size 36/38)
- felting sponge

a. If necessary, draw the design on a large sheet of paper first, filling the different areas with colour as a reference.

b. Hemming along both sides of one piece of hessian, redraw the design within a 92 x 38 cm (36 x 15 in) rectangle.

c. Using scissors and a fabric gauge when helpful, cut a variety of fabrics into prodding-sized pieces (see Preparation, page 34). Sort them into colours and tones, filling one transparent bag with a variety of pale neutral shades. Other bags should be filled with different colours and their various tones, for the other shapes.

d. Begin working with the spring-clip hook (see Techniques, page 40) by pulling a few different fabric pieces through appropriate areas of the design, as colour reminders. Continue filling in the shapes marked out on the hessian, ensuring that your spacing creates the desired thickness of pile. Create an adaptation of the 'mizzy-mazzy' effect, both in the neutral background and also within several shapes, by mixing the tones of each colour.

e. Once the rug is completed, place the other piece of hessian on top of the runner's reverse,

mark its outer shape and cut around it, leaving a reasonable excess all the way round for turning under and hemming.

f. Setting this aside, turn under 4 cm (1½ in) surplus hessian all the way around the runner, mitring the corners and concealing any excess. Spread the reverse and mitres with a thin layer of latex and allow it to dry for a few minutes. Repeat the process, again allowing drying time.

g. Position the hemmed hessian lining on the reverse of the runner and press the entire surface areas together. Allow this to dry overnight.

h. Adjust and trim the rug pile on the front surface where necessary, leaving it shaggier in some areas, slightly bevelling the sides, and clarifying the design's shapes.

i. Make approximately 16 felted balls in different sizes and colours. A combination of methods can be used, including wet-felting (see page 47 and step l. in the Lady Teacosy project on page 86).

j. Attach them, side by side, to each end of the runner's base cloth, using a crewel needle and a double length of woollen yarn.

12. Spotty lovebird cushion

A comfy cushion for the playroom floor or your living room sofa, this chirpy bird should make you feel like spring has sprung! The design could also be framed for a wall piece.

You will need:

- indelible marker pen
- tracing paper
- coloured pencils, transfer pencil, ruler
- pressing cloth, iron
- frame
- hessian to fit
- drawing pins or staple gun and staples
- rug hook
- scissors

- assorted colourful fabrics, including net, blanket wool, velvet and t-shirt cotton, cut into long strips, 1 cm (½ in) wide
- novelty and textured yarns
- needles, sewing threads, pins
- lining material, 66 cm (26 in) square
- colour co-ordinated canvas, 66 cm (26 in) square

- Velcro sew-on hook and loop tape, 38 cm (15 in)
- latex adhesive, spreader
- dyed fleece, red, yellow, orange and green
- felting needle, size 36/38
- felting sponge
- 9 shisha mirrors, button
- flexible wire or scoobies
- 56 cm (22 in) polyester-filled cushion pad

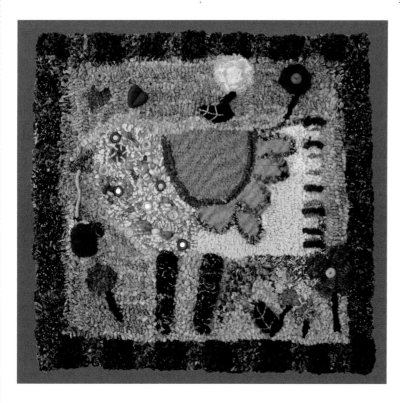

a. Follow step a. in the Hooked and braided rug instructions on page 79.

b. Attach the hessian tightly to your frame, ensuring that the 56 cm (22 in) square design is positioned centrally and not distorted.

c. Using four similarly toned fabrics, start to hook the squares along each side of the design with alternating colours, roughly matching opposite sides.

d. When hooking the bird's head, leave small spaces for the mirrors and eye to be stitched, and also for the fleece sculpted areas.

e. This area can be worked in a patterned fabric, with thick woollen yarn to chain-hook a few lines within the hooked loops, to emphasise the bird's shape (see Techniques, page 41).

f. Hook the outlines of the scalloped wings with novelty yarns.

g. Within the tail strip, create additional stripes with a number of raised wrapped wire loops (see Techniques, page 41), securing them through the hooking to the reverse of the design.

h. With a length of wire or scoobie, create the green flower stem similarly, determining its shape by couching it over the hooked area. Other stems can be hooked in green fabric, the loops being sheared.

i. Hook the background area within the border in a mainly lateral direction, to give the design some further contrast. Leave spaces for the felt heart and leaves to be applied.

j. Shear the loops of the hooked pink flower above the bird to create textural interest.

k. Use woollen blanket fabrics to hook the bird's legs and the flower in the bottom right of the design, carving and sculpting both afterwards (see Techniques, page 41). With the same treatment, use fleece strips for hooking the bulbous flower head.

l. Vary your hooking height in parts of the other flower, shearing some of the longer loops.

m. With a felting needle, dyed fleece and sponge (see Techniques, page 42), create the heart, flower, leaves and fleece sculpted centres. Decorate the leaves with stitched woollen detail. Stitch them all in place, shaping the heart by sewing down its centre tightly.

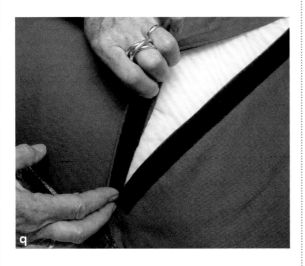

n. Remove the design from your frame, trimming the overlapping hessian to 5 cm (2 in) around the design and folding it to the back. Stitch this in place from the front, concealing any exposed hessian. Tidy excess loose threads and scoobies on the reverse side.

o. Apply latex thinly to the reverse surface, allowing it to dry overnight. Turning the edges of all four sides underneath, attach lining fabric using ladder stitch.

p. With a sturdy fabric, cut two pieces for the cushion back, measuring 32.5 x 53 cm (13 x 21 in) and 25 x 53 cm (10 x 21 in), plus extra for attaching Velcro and seam allowances. After the edges have been hemmed, machine a 45 cm (18 in) length of the hooked surface of Velcro along the inside of the larger piece of fabric, and the looped length to the outside of the smaller piece, ensuring that they correspond.

q. After turning in the edges along all sides, ladder stitch the smaller panel, then the larger one, in place, to form the back of the cushion. Insert the cushion pad, closing the fastening.

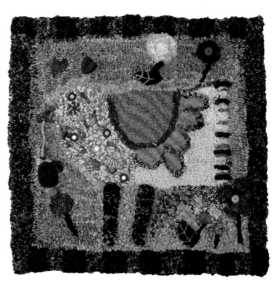

13. Tooth fairy pillow

Which little girl, on losing a tooth, would not be happy to hang this in her bedroom, or place it by her pillow, and await a visit from the tooth fairy?

You will need:

- tracing paper
- pencil, transfer pencil
- iron, pressing cloth
- drawing pins or staple gun and staples
- frame
- hessian, to fit
- indelible marker

- rug hook
- needles, threads
- latex adhesive, spreader
- scissors
- assorted fabrics, including gold and silver, cut into 0.5 cm (¼ in) strips
- assorted braids and trims, including net, sequins and ric-rac

- tiny coloured glass beads, silver bead or metallic coin
- pink braided piping cord, 109 cm (43 in) length
- wadding
- lining, 25 x 30 cm (10 x 12 in)
- woollen fabric, 25 x 30 cm (10 x 12 in)

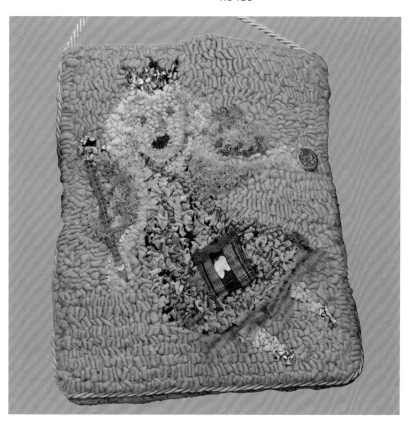

a. Repeat step a. of the Hooked and braided rug instructions on page 79, placing the design within an outer measurement of 24 x 28 cm (9 ½ x 11 in). Attach this to your frame, ensuring that the design is placed centrally and does not distort when stretching.

b. Use a blend of pink fabrics for hooking the tooth fairy's dress, and flesh tones for her face and arms.

c. Stitch either gathered net or net braid to decorate the bottom of the fairy's dress, and shear the loops of her wings once they have been hooked in a printed nylon.

d. Hook the fairy's hair finely in a range of yellow and ochre tones, and her crown and shoes in gold fabrics.

e. Fill in the details of her face carefully, matching slightly darker tones for the nose and face outline. With a fine pair of scissors, trim and adjust any details.

f. Use a soft but sturdy lilac fabric for the hooked even rows of background, ensuring that the fairy's shape is maintained.

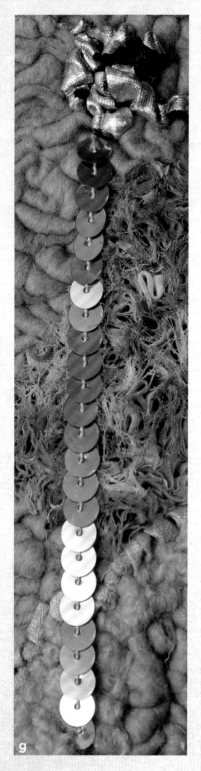

g. Hook a silver star, and complete the wand by using a 10 cm strip of sequinned braid, secured on the reverse side at each end.

h. Thread tiny beads for the fairy's necklace, securing again on the reverse, and stitch a bead or coin 'jewel' into place on her hand.

i. Make a small pocket for the dress in contrasting fabric, folding the excess fabric behind, and embellishing with a tooth shape cut from white fabric. Embellish further with a strip of ric-rac braid. Stitch the pocket into position on the hooked dress, leaving the top open for future tooth and coin deposits!

j. Leaving a hessian overlap of 2.5 cm (1 in) around the design, repeat steps n. and o. of the Spotty lovebird cushion instructions on page 94, as applicable.

k. Placing wadding between, and turning the excess fabric behind, stitch the lining fabric to the hessian just within the outer edge of the design.

l. Allowing sufficient for hanging the pillow, stitch the piping cord around three sides between the lining and the hooked design, leaving the top edge unpiped.

l.1

l.2

14. Tote bag

This bag makes an ideal child's shopper or a sleepover bag for packing pyjamas. However, it can also be scaled up for a larger tote bag. Because the bag is already made up and you are hooking onto a relatively rigid background, it can be worked freely on your lap without a frame. Use smooth and stretchy fabrics for hooking.

You will need:

- hessian tote bag (see Supplies and resources, page 124)
- card
- indelible marker
- rug hook
- scissors
- bodkin, needles, thread
- 3 coloured yarns

- sparkly patterned Lycra
- patterned and plain stretchy and woollen fabrics, cut into 1.5 cm (½ in) wide strips
- blue button
- curtain ring
- gold or metallic thread
- latex adhesive, spreader

a. Either draw the design onto the bag freehand or make templates of the bird and flower head and draw around them with a marker, placing the bird centrally on the bag front. Draw the remaining details, including the lettering, freehand or use a transfer pencil and tracing paper, as instructed in the Christmas stocking (page 63) and other projects.

b. Use strips of patterned stretchy fabric to hook the 'saddle' of the bird, working it concentrically from the outline inwards. Outline this shape with one row hooked in a darker plain fabric.

c. Hook the outlined details of the bird in a bright, plain fabric to stand out.

d. Hook the remainder of the bird's body, around and within these details, in a sparkly patterned Lycra to give the design some shimmer and glitz. Manipulate the details of the bird carefully into place as you proceed with the hooking.

e. The beak should be hooked using two tones of woollen fabric. Once completed, the beak's loops can be sheared to give it a contrasting texture.

a

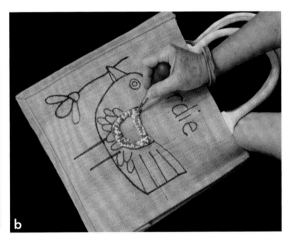

b

c

e

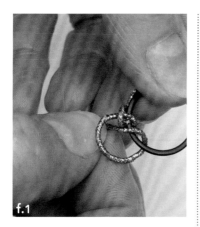

f.1

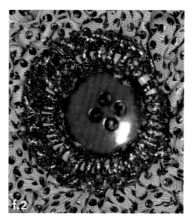

f.2

f. Make a lark's head knot around a curtain ring, using strong metallic thread (see technique in image above). Continue making knots until the ring is covered, tucking in the thread ends with a needle to secure. Stitch the button in place, and laying the gold ring over this, stitch it to complete the eye.

g. Chain-hook the lettering, flower stem and bird's legs (see Techniques, page 41). Use a different colour and texture of yarn for each of these sections.

h. Trim any loose ends and spread a thin layer of latex over the reverse of the hooked area of the bag. Stand the bag on its rectangular base and allow to dry overnight.

g

Community projects

8

As practised historically by families and neighbours on both sides of the Atlantic, larger-scale rag-rug projects can be ideally suited to a collaborative effort within a broad range of circumstances and settings. Perhaps the low cost, relative ease and rapid achievement level of the craft all help to make the medium attractive and accessible as a group venture.

Most larger rug frames will accommodate six people simultaneously working on a piece of work. This sort of group effort is usually very sociable and democratic, as well as having its obvious creative benefits. Perhaps because the hands are occupied with soothing and repetitive techniques, intimate conversation and the exchange of ideas are permitted and encouraged. In such a setting, I have known health and well-being information to be imparted, delicious recipes described and noted, and in the most natural and unselfconscious manner, counselling and support be both given and received.

Collaborative rag-rug projects can suit various stages of the school environment, where the end result might include the creation of a textile wall hanging to enhance a focal interior space within the building. Even the initial task of sourcing and sorting fabrics, which can involve many members of the school, can produce feelings of ownership of and inclusion in the work.

For primary-school classes, the medium can be an ideal way of addressing and including a broad range of cross-curricular themes. Aspects of literacy and science, such as the development and enrichment of vocabulary and descriptive language, plant and animal life, as well as design and technology, can be incorporated, whilst introducing the concept and handling of new tools, and the distinctions between natural and synthetic fibres.

59

59 Lynne Stein with Creative Minds, Eccleston, *Mats for the Millennium* *community textile project, 1999.* *Photograph by Lynne Stein.*

At the other end of the spectrum, the medium often has significance for elderly people, who may have memories of rag rugs and their tools, and the accompanying songs and stories, left over from childhood. The process of making a rag rug can provide a valuable parallel for, and access to, reminiscence work. In some parts of the country, where older volunteers provide support in schools, an intergenerational project can be very effective in building and enriching those special relationships.

Ways of working sometimes depend on the age and size of a group, and their ideas about the design of the final piece. There are situations where it might be more appropriate for individuals to make their own separate textiles on smaller frames. These could ultimately be stitched and joined together. Having a larger adult group than can be accommodated at the rug frame is not necessarily problematic, since some people are willing to switch their roles from session to session, or simply happy to be part of the group socially, whilst cutting up fabrics or making the tea. Others might create additional surfaces, such as beading and pompoms, for later embellishment.

Making a rag rug might provide a focus for issue-based work, where a group wish to formulate and express certain ideas and concerns. The process, appropriate for addressing issues of conflict resolution and encouraging interfaith dialogue, is also suited to many health-related situations, including hospital and health centre waiting areas and occupational therapy departments. Since it is such a very tactile medium, it also lends itself well to working with partially sighted people. The prodding technique, particularly, can effectively be used when working with individuals with learning disabilities. The work is stabilised on a frame, leaving both hands free to master the motion. Being able to make choices from a broad colour range of fabrics, and feeling their different weights and textures, is a vital part of the activity.

60 Lynne Stein, *Everyone Smiles in the Same Language,* 2011 onwards. Interfaith textile project. DVI children's dental clinic, Jerusalem. Photograph by Lynne Stein.

In primary-school projects, selecting predominantly smooth, stretchy, manageable fabrics, possibly sourced from t-shirts, leggings, knitwear and pyjamas, as well as providing an exciting vibrant palette, will be vital in making the task more enjoyable. The prodded technique is more suited to younger children, whereas 7–8-year-olds and upwards will usually master hooking.

As well as children's fiction, poems bearing strong visual imagery, such as those of Ted Hughes, Edward Lear and the cautionary verses of Hilaire Belloc, will lend themselves well to children's illustrations, and their subsequent translation into the medium, using both hooked and prodded techniques. Looking at the work of artists such as Clarice Cliff, Matisse and Hundertwasser, and their use of pattern, can provide a focus for individual hooked panels with 8–11-year-olds. Drawing and painting self-portraits and those of classmates, in the style of, say, Picasso, and observing facial expressions, colour and costume, can also be a good starting point for fabric work. For older design and technology pupils, a project could be based on the theme of underwater life, incorporating the preliminary processes of tie dye, batik and silk-painting, in preparation for making hooked panels for cushions or bags.

Within a busy waiting area in a children's clinic, the invitation to participate in creating a group 'work of art' which will eventually brighten up an otherwise dismal and unwelcoming treatment space, can alleviate anxiety and boredom while teaching a child exciting new skills. Possible themes are endless, ranging from the depiction of myths and fables, and cartoon characters, to using children's thoughts and feelings about visits to the doctor or dentist as the inspiration for primary artwork for a collaborative wall hanging.

Children's libraries also provide an opportunity to enhance the space with a vibrant and colourful rag rug. A mat, made for the children to sit on at story time, could also be hung on the wall for all to see. A library or public building might be just the place to display the visual storytelling of a local historical event, or the celebration of a significant centenary. The preliminary research for such a work can occupy all members of the group, as can decision-making about the eventual design.

61 **Lynne Stein with Gorse Covert Primary School**, *1997. 1.68 x 1.07 m (60 x 42 in)*. **Risley Moss Nature Reserve**, *Warrington*.

Gallery

9

As this book's title suggests, many of the following examples illustrate the huge potential for a graphic and painterly form of self-expression within the medium of rag-rugging; its capacity for experimentation and surface embellishment; and the diversity of approaches by different makers, whether they choose to create functional or decorative, traditional or contemporary works.

62 **Joan Moshimer,** *Two Lions*, *1997. 1.24 x 1.75 m (49 x 69 in). 100% wool. Hand-dyed. One of America's best-known and respected designers, makers and teachers of rug hooking. Having designed over four hundred in her lifetime, this was the last rug she completed before her death in 2000. Picture credit: Jesse Deupree. Photographer: Warren Roos.*

62

63

65

63 Barbara Klunder, *Listen Rug*, 1998. 66 x 114 cm (26 x 45 in).
*Barbara's strips of hooking material include all kinds of fabric, from
ribbons and t-shirts to ball gowns, in order to achieve her subtle
colour blends and clarity of form. Photographer: Jeremy Jones.*

64 Barbara Klunder, *Drum Rug*, 1998. 66 x 114 cm (26 x 45 in).

65 Louisa Creed, *Cat*, 1990. 81 x 69 cm (32 x 27 in). *Mixed
recycled materials. Louisa's original sketch was squared up 4:1 to
enlarge it for the rug. Experimental with her colours, she has given the
cat expression with unexpected tones and textures.
Photographer: John Worrallo.*

66 Lewis Creed, *Happy Dog*, 2009. 56 x 56 cm (22 x 22 in). *Mixed
recycled materials. Using a latch hook, Lewis' simple joyful design has
a graphic, cartoon-like appearance.
Photographer: John Worrallo.*

67

68

67 Kaisa Takala, Minna Piironen, & Hanna-Liisa Pykala, *Postcard from Helsinki*, 2010. 3.5 x 6 m (138 x 236 in). A temporary piece of exterior art in Helsinki, consisting of twenty-two thousand knots, using durable recycled plastics and building mesh; made by Finnish design students as an expression of love for Helsinki people, and as a welcome to tourists.

68 Emma Tennant, *Geraniums*, 2008. 61 x 89 cm (24 x 35 in). Also a painter and gardener, Emma's horticultural imagery and skilful juxtaposition of plain, tweed and twill fabrics give her rugs a distinctive appearance. Copyright: Hermitage Rugs/Emma Tennant. Photographer: Katie Pertwee.

69 Jennifer Manuell, *Gossip*, *2006. 23 x 30 x 5 cm (9 x 12 x 2 in). A Canadian fourth-generation rug hooker, Jennifer combines predominantly space-dyed yarns and self-dyed woollen fabrics to create the rich flora and fauna designs in her handbags.*

70 Julia Burrowes, **Diamonds**, *early 1990s. 13 x 8 cm (5 x 3 in). Spring hooked, worked on rug canvas. Julia's training as a painter is evident in her use of colour on this geometric clipped rug. Fascinated by old quilts and rag rugs, she uses largely reclaimed woollen fabrics, concerned with their concealed history.*

71

71 Brandon Mably, Mischievous Cat, *1996. 86 cm x 1.04 m (34 x 41 in). Brandon loves searching for fabrics at charity shops and car boot sales. Hooked loosely, the design and palette for this beautiful rug enhance the artefacts and furnishings within its interior. Picture credit: The Kaffe Fassett Studio. Featured in* Glorious Interiors *(London: Ebury Press, 1995).*

72

73

72 Kaffe Fassett, *Mosaic*. *78 x 120 cm (31 x 47 in). Enjoying the vibrant colour and textural potential afforded by the medium, Kaffe's mosaic design is worked with a latch hook, using thrift shop fabrics. Comparable to traditional 'crazy paving' rag-rug patterns, the grey outlines in Mosaic give unity to the whole design. Picture credit: The Kaffe Fassett Studio. Featured in* Glorious Interiors *(London: Ebury Press, 1995).*

73 Linda Rae Coughlin, *Walking on Eggs*, *2007. 38 x 43 cm (15 x 17 in). Hooked, stitched, machine and hand embroidered. Recycled fabrics, linen foundation, threads, gold chain. Linda combines rag-rug techniques, embroidery and artefacts to make political and personal gender statements, which can sometimes be uncomfortable, but always powerful.*

74 Lu Mason, P.J.B, *1986. 152 x 91 cm (5 x 3 ft). Wool on hessian. Inspired by 50s fabrics and plates, African prints, and 20s and 30s Russian painted china. Tweeds and brightly coloured fabrics, black outlines and decorative pattern are used to great effect in Lu's designs.*

75 Prunella Bramwell-Davies, *The Inside and Outside Are One,* 2008. 51 x 61 cm (20 x 24 in). Hooked cotton and mixed fibres. Shading and volume are successfully achieved by the compact hooking and closely blended fabric tones. Photographer: Ian Hessenberg.

76 Rachelle Leblanc, *Under Watchful Eyes,* 2011. 69 x 74 cm (27 x 29 in). A Canadian artist, Rachelle's approach owes much to her passion for painting, textiles and rug hooking. Her themes are personal, often recapturing childhood memories. Latch-hooked on linen backing cloth, to obtain Rachelle's distinctive palette with her self-dyed 100% wool and cashmere fabric strips.

75

76

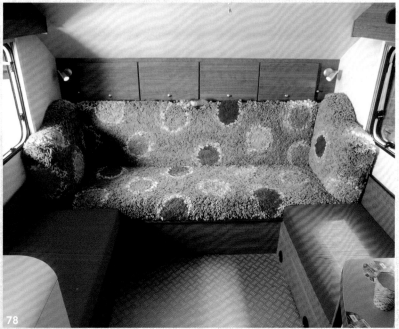

77 **Trish Little,** *MeMe Mat,* 2000. 45 cm x 10.8 m (18 in x 35 ft). Largely recycled assorted fabrics hooked into hessian. Trish's work, sometimes taking on a three-dimensional form, is often a passionate response to political issues, and the wide open spaces of the West Australian Goldfields area where she lives. Photographer: Gary Blinco.

78 **Ali Rhind,** *Sofabed,* 2005. Using mainly woollen self-dyed blankets to prod boldly patterned fabric, perfectly suited to upholstery, this was made for a caravan as part of the celebratory touring exhibition 'Trailer Made', in collaboration with Designed&Made, Newcastle. Photographer: David Lawson.

79 **Lynne Stein, Mythological Beast,**
1998. 56 x 56 cm (22 x 22 in). Hand-
hooked, wrapped wire, stitched.
Largely recycled fabrics, fibres and
embellishments. Inspired by fairy tales,
mythology and pantomime. Property of
Tamara Schneck.

80 **Lynne Stein, *Cabbages and Lots of Flowers*** (detail), 2009. 1.09 x 1.04 m (43 x 41 in). Gun-tufted, needle felted, wrapped wire, stitched. Largely recycled fabrics and fibres, polyester backing cloth. Inspired by local allotments, their patterns and symmetry.

81 **Sara Worley, *Spot Rug*,** 2009. 90 x 60 cm (35 x 24 in). Hooked, upcycled mixed fabrics. The colours and bold contemporary graphic imagery in this rug have a retro quality.

Museum and gallery collections

10

United Kingdom

Abbott Hall, Museum of Lakeland Life, Cumbria
American Museum, Bath
Beamish Open Air Museum, Northumberland
Black Country Living Museum, West Midlands
Cromer Museum, Norfolk
Eyemouth Museum, Whitby
Fife Folk Museum
Grace Darling Museum, Northumberland
Grosvenor Museum, Chester
Guernsey Folk Museum
Highland Folk Museum, Inverness
Ironbridge Gorge Museum (Blists Hill), Shropshire
King's Lynn Museum, Norfolk
Manx National Heritage Museum, Isle of Man
National Mining Museum of Scotland, Midlothian
National Waterways Museum, Ellesmere Port
Old Merchant's House, Great Yarmouth
Ryedale Folk Museum, North Yorkshire
Scottish Fisheries Museum, Anstruther
Shipley Art Gallery, Gateshead
Stromness Museum, Orkney
Tullie House Museum, Carlisle
Ulster Folk and Transport Museum, Northern Ireland
Upper Dales Folk Museum, North Yorkshire
Victoria & Albert Museum, London
Welsh Folk Museum, Cardiff
Woodhorn Colliery Museum, Northumberland
Yorkshire Museum of Farming, York

USA

Billings Farm and Museum, Woodstock, Vermont
Coutts Memorial Museum of Art, California
Creative Growth Art Center, California
Henry Ford Museum, Michigan
Heritage Center of Lancaster County, Pennsylvania
Huntington Museum of Art, West Virginia
Museum of American Folk Art, New York
Rhode Island School of Design Museum
Shaker Museum, New York
Shelburne Museum, Vermont
Wenham Historical Museum, Massachusetts

Canada

Art Gallery of Nova Scotia, Halifax
Canadian Craft Museum, Vancouver
Canadian Museum of Civilisation, Quebec
Cheticamp Hooked Rugs, Nova Scotia
McCord Museum of Canadian History, Montreal
New Brunswick Museum, Newfoundland
North American Hooked Rug Museum, Nova Scotia
Royal Ontario Museum, Toronto
Textile Museum of Canada, Toronto

Australia

Historic Houses Trust, New South Wales
Powerhouse Museum, Sydney

Further reading

Boswell, Thom (ed.), *The Rug Hook Book*
(New York, USA: Sterling, 1992)

Reakes, Lizzie, *Ragwork*
(London: Lorenz Books, 1996)

Vail, Juju, *Rag Rugs*
(London: Apple, 1997)

Bawden, Juliet, *Rag Rug Inspirations*
(London: Cassell, 1996)

Davies, Ann, *How to Make Hand-Hooked Rag Rugs*
(Tunbridge Wells: Search Press, 1996)

Davies, Ann, *Rag Rugs*
(London: Letts, 1992)

Hubbard, Clare, *Making Rag Rugs*
(Massachusetts, USA: Storey Books, 2002)

Pulido, Theresa, *Hook, Loop and Lock*
(Ohio, USA: Krause Publications, 2009)

Hinchcliffe, John and Jeffs, Angela, *Rugs from Rags*
(London: Orbis Publishing, 1977)

Reeves, Sue, *Country Rag Crafts*
(Newton Abbott: David & Charles, 1996)

Meany, Janet and Pfaff, Paula, *Rag Rug Handbook*
(Colorado, USA: Interweave Press, 1996)

Kopp, Joel and Kate, *American Hooked and Sewn Rugs*
(New York, USA: E.P. Dutton & Co. Inc., 1975)

Tennant, Emma, *Rag Rugs of England and America*
(London: Walker Books, 1992)

Winthrop Kent, William, *The Hooked Rug*
(New York, USA: Tudor Publishing, 1937)

Allan, Rosemary E., *From Rags to Riches: North
Country Rag Rugs* (County Durham: Beamish North
of England Open Air Museum, 2007)

Conversion chart

Metric		Imperial
2.5 centimetres (cm)	=	1 inch (in)
90 centimetres	=	1 yard (yd)
1 metre (m)	=	39 inches

Supplies and resources

UK

Fred Aldous
37 Lever Street
Manchester M1 1LW
0161 236 4224
www.fredaldous.co.uk
(textile and craft supplies)

Jenni Stuart-Anderson
The Birches
Middleton-on-the-Hill
Herefordshire HR6 0HN
www.jenni.ragrugs.freeuk.com
(workshops, rug making)

Iriss of Penzance
66 Chapel Street
Penzance
Cornwall TR18 4AD
01736 366568
www.iriss.co.uk
(rug making, felting)

Ragart Studios
2 New Row
Pontrhydygroes
Ystrad Meurig
Ceredigion
Wales SY25 6DT
www.ragartstudios.com
(workshops, rug making)

Rainbow Silks
6 Wheelers Yard
High Street
Great Missenden
Bucks HP16 0AL
01494 862111
www.rainbowsilks.co.uk
(workshops, textile supplies)

Debbie Siniska
www.debbiesiniska.co.uk
(workshops, rug making)

Lynne Stein
01565 632595
www.lynnestein.com
(workshops, rug making, felting)

Texere Yarns
College Mill
Barkerend Road
Bradford BD1 4AU
www.texere-yarns.co.uk
(textile supplies)

The Clever Baggers
0845 2600 393
www.thecleverbaggers.co.uk
(jute tote bags)

George Weil
Old Portsmouth Road
Peasmarsh
Guildford
Surrey GU3 1LZ
01483 565800
www.georgeweil.com
(textile and craft supplies)

Wingham Wool Work
70 Main Street
Wentworth
Rotherham
South Yorkshire S62 7TN
01226 742926
www.winghamwoolwork.co.uk
(felting, dyes)

USA

W. Cushing and Company
Box 351 Kennebunkport
ME 04046
(207) 467 3745
www.wcushing.com
(rug making, dyes)

Green Mountain Hooked Rugs
2838 County Road
Montpelier
Vermont 05602
(802) 223 1333
www.greenmountainhookedrugs.com
(rug making, dyes, classes)

Halcyon Yarn
12 School Street
Bath
ME 04530
www.halcyonyarn.com
(rug making, felting, dyes, classes)

Lakeside Oaks Rug Hooking
2727 Campbell Drive
Auburn
CA 95602
www.iloverughooking.com
(rug making, dyes, classes)

Searsport Rug Hooking
7548 Ratan Circle
Port Charlotte
FL 33981
www.searsportrughooking.com
(rug making, dyes)

Yankee Peddler
267 Route 81
Killingworth
CT 06419
(860) 663 0526
www.yankeepeddler.com
(rug making)

CANADA

Deanne Fitzpatrick
33 Church Street
Amherst
Nova Scotia
B4H 3A7
1 800 328 7756
www.hookingrugs.com
(rug making, classes)

Legacy Studio
212 West Terrace Point
Cochrane
Alberta
T4C 1S1
1 866 932 0932
www.legacystudio.ca
(rug making, felting, dyes)

LinArt Designs
Linda D Ferretti
3773 Highway 203
RR1 Shelburne
Nova Scotia
BOT 1WO
902 875 4175
www.linartdesigns.com
(rug making, dyes)

Moose River Rug Hooking Studio
14 Clementsport Road
Clementsport
Nova Scotia
B0S 1E0
902 638 3200
www.mooseriverstudio.com
(rug making, classes)

Rittermere-Hurst-Field
P.O. Box 487
Aurora
Ontario L4G 3L6
1 800 268 9813
www.letshookrugs.com
(rug making, dyes, classes)

AUSTRALIA

Fibre Fusion
P.O. Box 67 Kew East
Victoria 3102
613 9859 8081
www.fibrefusion.com.au
(felting)

Studio Blue
20 Langhorne Creek Road
Strathalbyn 5255
61 08 8536 3451
www.ausrugcrafters.com
(rug making, workshops)

GUILDS AND SOCIETIES

Association of Traditional Hooking
Artists
www.atharugs.com

Australian Rug Makers Guild
www.rughookingaustralia.com.au

The International Guild of
Handhooking Rugmakers
www.tighr.net

The Textile Society
0207 923 0331
www.textilesociety.org.uk

DIRECTORIES

The Rug Hookers Network
www.rughookersnetwork.com

The Textile and Fibre Art List
www.tafalist.com

JOURNALS

Hooking Matters
(The International Guild of
Handhooking Rugmakers' quarterly
newsletter)
www.tighr.net

Rug Hooking Magazine
www.rughookingmagazine.com

The Wool Street Journal
www.woolstreetjournal.com

SOCIAL ENTERPRISES,
CO-OPERATIVES,
COLLECTIONS

www.berber-arts.com
www.creativegrowth.org
www.mielie.com
www.rug-aid.org
www.rughookproject.com

Acknowledgements

Unless otherwise stated, and apart from those in the Gallery section of this book, which if uncredited, were photographed by the artists, all photographs in this book have been taken by Robbie Wolfson.

I should like to express my thanks to my editor, Agnes Upshall, for her continual positivity and encouragement. I am also indebted to Ali Rhind, who is partially responsible for 'getting me hooked' in the first place! My thanks and appreciation to the numerous contributors, for the beautiful examples of their work in this book. I am specifically grateful to the following people, all of whom in different ways have given me their generous help: Charlotte Bell, Linda Berman, Gebhart Blazek, Lisette Bourgeois, Siegrun Brunt, Jesse Deupree, The Hidden Jem, Grace Flinn, Helen Flynn, Anne and Malvin Flynn, Melanie Gardner (Tullie House Museum and Art Gallery), Penny Godfrey, Jennifer Gordon (Scottish Fisheries Museum), Karen Griffiths, Iwona Hetherington (Powerhouse Museum), Sue Mosco, Maureen Morano, Jovan Nicholson, Joel Stein, Shelagh Wolfson, and to Mercedes Yau and Eloise Shneck, supermodels extraordinaires! Last, but never least, my thanks go to my husband, Robbie Wolfson, for his photographic skills and patience, and for his unstinting love and support.

About the author

Lynne Stein originally trained as an exhibition and display designer, and also as an art therapist. She is a self-taught textile artist, living in Cheshire, and runs a variety of textile workshops, both privately and in educational and healthcare settings, museums and galleries. Lynne's work has for the past 25 years been widely exhibited, and she has undertaken commissions both within and beyond the UK, for a wide range of public, corporate and domestic spaces. As well as in books and magazines, she has been featured on BBC TV and radio broadcasts including Radio 2's Home Front. In 2012, Lynne ran a successful community project with AgeUK to create a rug in honour of the Queen's Diamond Jubilee. She also runs an ongoing interfaith community textile project in a children's dental clinic in Jerusalem.

www.lynnestein.com

Index